D0630130

Strategic Global Sourcing
Best Practices

Strategic Global Sourcing
Best Practices

FRED SOLLISH, MS
JOHN SEMANIK, MBA

WILEY

John Wiley & Sons, Inc.

Copyright © 2011 by John Wiley & Sons, Inc. All rights reserved.

Published by John Wiley & Sons, Inc., Hoboken, New Jersey.
Published simultaneously in Canada.

No part of this publication may be reproduced, stored in a retrieval system, or
transmitted in any form or by any means, electronic, mechanical, photocopying,
recording, scanning, or otherwise, except as permitted under Section 107 or 108 of the
1976 United States Copyright Act, without either the prior written permission of the
Publisher, or authorization through payment of the appropriate per-copy fee to the
Copyright Clearance Center, Inc., 222 Rosewood Drive, Danvers, MA 01923, (978)
750-8400, fax (978) 646-8600, or on the Web at www.copyright.com. Requests to the
Publisher for permission should be addressed to the Permissions Department, John
Wiley & Sons, Inc., 111 River Street, Hoboken, NJ 07030, (201) 748-6011, fax (201)
748-6008, or online at www.wiley.com/go/permissions.

Limit of Liability/Disclaimer of Warranty: While the publisher and author have used their
best efforts in preparing this book, they make no representations or warranties with
respect to the accuracy or completeness of the contents of this book and specifically
disclaim any implied warranties of merchantability or fitness for a particular purpose. No
warranty may be created or extended by sales representatives or written sales materials.
The advice and strategies contained herein may not be suitable for your situation. You
should consult with a professional where appropriate. Neither the publisher nor author
shall be liable for any loss of profit or any other commercial damages, including but not
limited to special, incidental, consequential, or other damages.

For general information on our other products and services or for technical support,
please contact our Customer Care Department within the United States at (800)
762-2974, outside the United States at (317) 572-3993 or fax (317) 572-4002.

Wiley also publishes its books in a variety of electronic formats. Some content that
appears in print may not be available in electronic books. For more information about
Wiley products, visit our web site at www.wiley.com.

Library of Congress Cataloging-in-Publication Data:

Sollish, Fred.
  Strategic global sourcing best practices / Fred Sollish, John Semanik.
    p. cm.
Includes index.
  ISBN 978-0-470-49440-0 (hardback); ISBN 978-0-470-94928-3 (ebk);
  ISBN 978-0-470-94929-0 (ebk); ISBN 978-0-470-94930-6 (ebk)
  1. Industrial procurement. 2. Purchasing. 3. Strategic planning. 4. Business
logistics. I. Semanik, John. II. Title.
  HD39.5.S664 2011
  658.7′2–dc22

                                                                        2010037969

Printed in the United States of America

10 9 8 7 6 5 4 3 2 1

Contents

Preface

For most of its history, procurement has been focused primarily on transactional processing, with virtually no strategic decision-making responsibilities. The typical purchasing routine has been simple: receive a requisition from the user, place the purchase order with the supplier, expedite when necessary, and resolve invoice discrepancies. In this process, there was very little room for decision making such as supply sourcing and even less for discretion. Furthermore, it has been widely estimated that even as late as the 1990s, less than 60 percent of an organization's spending with suppliers was controlled by any part of the procurement organization.

Today, this is certainly no longer the case; procurement has evolved into a strategic element in the competitive arsenal of most organizations. There is now a justifiable movement toward centralized control of corporate spending for cost reduction, compliance, and risk management. In fact, many U.S. organizations now mandate that *all* external spending come under the auspices and control of the procurement or supply management group.

What created this change? We can only surmise. Competitive pressure to reduce costs most likely has a large role; Sarbanes-Oxley legislation requiring the disclosure of risks to shareholders may also contribute. And as executive management's awareness of procurement's potential to positively impact the profitability of the organization evolved, the level of professionalism within the procurement group has improved as well. Twenty years ago, no more than five universities offered graduate degrees in procurement, contract management, or supply management; now there are dozens in the United States alone. The trend points to a sustained increase in demand for educational opportunities in this field.

Recently, an even newer trend has emerged: the division and migration of the procurement/supply management group into strategic and tactical elements. Procurement has developed as a valuable tactical element, overseeing the day-to-day logistics operations with the supply base, while a new element in the procurement process, sourcing, has taken the longer-range, strategic role: finding, qualifying, developing, and contracting with domestic and global supply organizations. Keep in mind that sourcing is still in its relative infancy (although we hear so much about it). Because the process will likely continue to evolve substantially in the coming decade, it becomes difficult to forecast its ultimate evolution.

We will leave the future to visionaries. We chose to address in our review what we believe is the strategic sourcing state of the art at this time. Our task is one of surveying current practices in an attempt to uncover and document what we believe to be the best practices in sourcing operations. And since we are now facing an increasingly integrated world economy, we've tried to sift out those practices that apply globally as well.

We recognize that defining best practices is going to be somewhat subjective, based on the information we can gather and the opinions of others as well as our own. We say this with no attempt to excuse ourselves should we fail to pinpoint each and every one of the areas that come into the picture. Our task, we believe, is to provide the global supply professional with a basis for understanding sourcing practices as they exist today and to be informed enough to understand their evolution in the future.

In the sincere belief that we have accomplished this task, we invite you to join us in the strategic sourcing evolution.

Fred Sollish   John Semanik
San Francisco, California   San Jose, California

CHAPTER 1

An Overview of Global Strategic Sourcing

Although it has a grandiose-sounding title, strategic sourcing has its roots in very humble beginnings. Sourcing has always been a purchasing and supply management function. In its traditional form, it is the process of locating and employing suppliers. However, various organizations and academics often define this process in different ways when managing their supply chains. As supply chains extend into global markets today, we find under the heading of strategic sourcing a number of often confusing and disparate methods. We expect, in the pages that follow, to bring some measure of clarity to the subject. This chapter provides an overview of the topics we intend to cover in more detail in chapters that follow.

So let's begin our exploration with a basic definition, as we see it, to help keep us in alignment as we go through the more detailed processes in this book. Here is our definition:

> *Strategic sourcing is an organizational procurement and supply management process used to locate, develop, qualify, and employ suppliers that add maximum value to the buyer's products or services.*

> *The major objective of strategic sourcing is to engage suppliers that align with the strategic business and operational goals of the organization. We apply the term "strategic" to recognize that many sourcing projects require a long-term plan of supply chain action. It's meeting the needs of this relatively long time horizon that makes sourcing "strategic."*

> *When the word "global" is added to the title, it means that suppliers may be selected beyond the organization's national borders.*

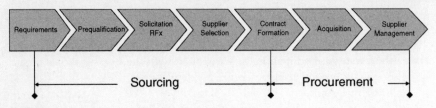

FIGURE 1.1 The Sourcing and Procurement Process

Using a thorough, comprehensive process to select suppliers is a path to organizational supply chain management excellence. But this is not an easy task at all. The suppliers we select must be able to lower overall cost, expedite time to market, reduce business risk, improve product or service quality, and support us through flexible scheduling and, possibly, production and engineering support.

Strategic sourcing does *not* include the day-to-day activities of the acquisition process. It does *not* include supplier's individual quotations, routine buying activities, logistics, quality assessment, performance analysis, and payment. Essentially, strategic sourcing and procurement part ways following the formation of a contract or the formal qualification of a selected supplier.

Figure 1.1 shows the typical supply management process starting with receipt of a request (requirements) through managing the supplier or contract.

The Strategic Sourcing Plan

When in place and understood by all stakeholders, a strategic sourcing plan provides guidance to those responsible for implementing acquisition policy. As with any plan, it should be well documented and systematically refer to the organizational mission and vision statements. The plan must also clearly take into account customer requirements that are identified in the organization's broader strategic business plan.

Plan Elements

Many organizations use a standard format in which to create departmental strategic plans. This uniformity helps when various plans are consolidated, since each of the plan elements are treated in a similar order. It also helps to ensure that critical path segments are not overlooked.

The common elements of a strategic plan can be outlined as described in the next subsections.

MISSION AND VISION   Traditionally, any strategic plan begins with a statement of mission and vision. The mission statement must set the tone for the objectives within the plan. The strategic sourcing plan should also contain a mission statement, and it should clearly align with the organization's business mission statement. It also needs to identify what value will be added by the sourcing group.

It is equally important to communicate the statement to all cross-functional departmental personnel. Most internal organizations work dutifully to create the plan and then place the document on a shelf. Very few cross-functional personnel outside of those who have contributed to the plan even know it exists. On one recent occasion, one of our authors recalls asking the chief executive officer (CEO) of a company he worked for to describe the organization's objectives. "Sorry," the CEO said. "That information is confidential."

> Do *you* know your organization's mission statement? It's not surprising to find that very few employees know, much less understand, the mission of their organization. In class after class, the authors asked how many attending knew their organization's mission statement well enough to recite it. We considered it fortunate to find more than two in any class of thirty-plus.

ENVIRONMENTAL ANALYSIS   An environmental analysis is another traditional element of the strategic sourcing plan. The environmental analysis describes current conditions within the organization as well as with its primary customers, its supply chain, and the overall market or industry. This analysis provides the background against which the plan is developed. Its importance lies in tying objectives to current business conditions; if conditions change significantly, the plan may require revision.

In our analysis, we must also take into account conditions across the entire supply chain that can impact our supply strategy. If we are a semiconductor manufacturer, we must consider our customers' demand for advanced technology and time our development process to coincide with their plans and technology roadmaps.

SWOT ANALYSIS   The plan should include a comprehensive SWOT (strengths, weaknesses, opportunities, and threats) analysis, traditionally used to guide plan implementers toward defining objectives. A SWOT analysis helps identify potential roadblocks (weaknesses and threats) and prepares the way for dealing with them through organizational strengths. It can also identify potential opportunities that help to implement the plan strategy. In the strategic sourcing plan, it is important to identify roadblock conditions since they invariably affect meeting key objectives. In fact, it is probably a good idea to describe all objectives as they relate to the SWOT analysis.

ASSUMPTIONS   Although it is ideal to have all of the detail needed to formulate the plan, this is rarely the case. Market dynamics will continue to change throughout the plan's period, and new conditions will arise that are unlikely to be foreseen. So what isn't clearly known or capable of forecast needs to be assumed so that the plan can go forward. These assumptions must be documented since, just as with environmental conditions, they are used as "just-in-case" placeholders. When we can replace assumptions with known facts, we can then make whatever adjustments to the plan that are required.

OBJECTIVES   Within the strategic sourcing plan, we can outline specific business objectives that we expect to achieve. Objectives, as we use the term here, are the expression of specific targets that will advance our mission by adding value to the organization. They are tied to the overall mission statement and take into account environmental conditions, our SWOT analysis, and any assumptions we make.

The plan describes objectives in clear and directive language. For example, our customers may be demanding environmentally friendly products. Do we need to move more aggressively into a green sourcing program?

When developing objectives, it's important to include measurements that go along with them. If you can't measure it, how will you know when you have achieved it?

Obviously, not all goals are of equal importance, and we know that in many cases, our resources will be limited, so it's important to prioritize all goals. Those that are most important are given the highest priority for achievement. We can also consider any objectives that can be achieved without using significant resources, perhaps in the course of fulfilling our general responsibilities.

Objectives for a strategic sourcing plan might include (as examples):

- A specific amount of cost saving
- An improvement in customer support through reduced lead times from suppliers and better on-time delivery performance
- Development of new supplier alliances and partnerships
- Reduction of inventory levels through, for example, consignment
- Development of new demand management planning tools and models

STRATEGY   Sourcing strategy must be developed within the scope of the overall mission statement and ensure, to the extent possible, achieving our objectives. For example: "We will actively support the organization's 'first to market' objectives." This simple statement can then be used to create a strategy. First to market may require Early Supplier Involvement (ESI). This in turn may generate the need for close alliances with key suppliers so that we can develop early involvement. (Early involvement is rather difficult if we are competing all of our purchases and can make an award only once the bids are analyzed.) For the sourcing team, strong business alliances as opposed to full bidding competition on all purchases, for example, represent a distinct strategy.

We must also ensure that our strategy addresses developments through-out the supply chain; it may be economic conditions, or it may be category or commodity shortages that escalate market pricing. We may have solid data, or we may need to make some critical assumptions. If we forecast an economic downturn, for example, we will likely want to reduce inventory in our suppliers' inventory pipelines.

Within the plan, we must initially identify cross-functional team members and describe their key roles and responsibilities. Particularly important are responsibilities for supplier negotiations and analysis for implementation; that is, developing and interpreting relevant data, and implementing actions such analysis generates. These efforts will likely be parsed out to existing commodity teams, so we will want to determine if we have the right people in the right places at the right time.

IMPLEMENTATION Keep in mind that the strategic sourcing plan establishes a high-level approach that does not delve into the details of tactical methods. So to implement our strategy, we require an operational strategy and a tactical approach to achieving our goals. This begins with an operational analysis that serves to bridge the strategic plan and the operational tactical plan.

Opportunity Analysis

The strategic sourcing plan needs to address procurement commodities or categories where potential opportunities for improvement have been identified. Improvements can take the form of lower prices, better quality, reduced inventory, and so on. We develop these through an opportunity analysis, typically an extension of the overall sourcing plan into areas managed by commodity or category groups. This analysis should be conducted by a cross-functional strategic sourcing team, preferably before finalizing the plan.

The opportunity analysis often uses industry benchmarks to determine where gaps exist between best practices and current practices in our organization. (We outline the gap analysis methodology in the next section.)

These benchmarks, developed by spend commodity, category, or industry, take into account our total annual volume (past and projected) so that we can be sure they are relevant in scope. We also need to know our historical experience with price increases within the commodity or with a specific supplier and what earlier cost and price improvements have been made.

The opportunity analysis and the benchmarking process are often by-products of the market analysis (which we address in Chapter 5) that takes place prior to the development of the strategic plan. Keep in mind that a significant number of opportunities may have been identified subsequent to the previous strategic sourcing plan, but we are, for now, interested only in those opportunities that align with the organization's objectives. Based on the data gathered through our opportunity analysis, we should be able to project the degree to which our plan will support the overall organizational plan.

Typically, the opportunity analysis will cover several elements:

- **Determine how and with whom we are spending our funds.** Known as spend analysis, this process reviews the organization's detailed spending history as a means to finding common items that can be consolidated by using fewer suppliers. The added volume for the suppliers we do use should provide additional price reduction negotiation opportunities.
- **Review spending history to find multiple items that are very similar and can be respecified to a single item.** We refer to this as part standardization or value engineering, and, as with spending analysis, we can leverage the larger consolidated spend as a way to generate price reductions. This is an especially productive area when the organization operates from multiple locations or when a merger or acquisition occurs.
- **Identify poor supplier performance.** Especially in areas that directly support the organization's mission, we should review suppliers' history to pinpoint those that are well below our expectations. Later we can determine if improvement is possible or if any supplier(s) need to be replaced.

    In relation to performance, we want to review (and perhaps benchmark) the measurements we use to assess supplier performance via a "scorecard." Is the supplier still relevant? Do our supplier metrics provide an accurate picture of how well the supplier is meeting our needs? And, perhaps more important, are we monitoring the supplier for contract compliance and performance to agreed-on service levels?
- **Improve competition.** Do important elements of our procurement strategies lack robust competition? Do suppliers of these items routinely raise prices regardless of market conditions? Do we have suppliers who believe they are sure to continue to receive our business regardless of

business conditions? Do we have products or services that have not been supply competed for several years? A "yes" to any of these questions may mean that we need to reformulate our supply strategy for achieving the best value from these suppliers as a reward for earning our business.

- **Investigate outsourcing opportunities.** Outsourcing, in general, and Business Process Outsourcing (BPO) specifically, is a well-established, significant component of strategic sourcing. As its title implies, the focus of BPO is on services. Some of the more commonly outsourced services include information technology (although often assigned to its own category), accounts payable, customer support, legal services, design and engineering, research and data analysis, logistics, security, facilities management, financial services, and procurement itself. The primary objectives of outsourcing are relatively clear: reduced cost through lower wages for labor, an extension of the organization's capabilities, a more specialized workforce, greater spend visibility, up-to-date technology, temporary personnel (and recruiting) and, importantly, the ability to meet variable demand without having to add employees.

  In addition to business processes, organizations are also engaged in outsourcing elements of manufacturing. In fact, electronic manufacturing services under subcontracts are likely the earliest example of outsourcing, tracing their roots to the traditional "make-or-buy" practice that would determine if a manufactured part or a manufacturing process could be converted to a purchase. Oddly enough, in the early days of assembly line manufacturing, vertical integration—that is, incorporating all elements of the end product's production within the company—was the rule rather than the exception.

  The outsourcing opportunity analysis should take into account geographical considerations, including the pros and cons of offshoring (outsourcing to companies based in other countries) or nearshoring (outsourcing to companies within the organization's national borders). Some aspects to consider in globalizing sourcing activities are the complexity and costs of currency exchange rates, taxes, transportation, and logistics (including Customs), overcoming cultural and language differences, and the risk factors inherent in the local economy and geopolitical climate. (Outsourcing is covered in more detail in Chapter 12.)

- **Capture additional spending.** It is not uncommon for organizations to tolerate spending by any number of departments without procurement involvement, sometimes called "maverick spending." Capturing this spending by the sourcing and procurement teams can lead to a number of benefits for the organization, such as improved pricing through negotiation, better value through competitive bidding, and tighter control of supplier performance. Capturing this spending also can

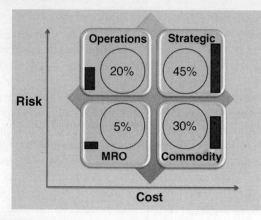

FIGURE 1.2 Supply Positioning

assist the sourcing and procurement group in achieving strategic supply savings goals.

- **Improve internal processes.** In many cases, opportunity means "work." Organizations sometimes find themselves in the peculiar position of having more cost-saving opportunities than there are staff members to implement them. However, if we can find ways to improve our internal procurement process, it's possible that we can free up resources to engage in cost savings or standardization projects. As an example, Figure 1.2 shows that our model allocates 5 percent of its spending (in dollars) to the MRO (Maintenance, Repair, and Operations), or Indirect, category. But in actual procurement volume, this category would likely account for nearly 50 percent of the ordering volume. Do we really want to allocate 50 percent of our staff to 5 percent of the spending?

During one recent assignment, our consulting team discovered a similar situation to the one outlined earlier. In developing a spending analysis, it was found that the MRO category accounted for about 8 percent of the procurement spend, with just over 45 percent of the transactions. Half the procurement staff (eight buyers) was allocated to this category of spend. Automating this very-low-risk category produced significant savings. The "liberated" team members went on to assist commodity groups in harvesting the identified savings possibilities.

By now, many organizations recognize the value gained by using purchasing cards. P-cards virtually eliminate the need to generate a purchase order since the card issuer can provide detailed spending reports that can be approved by management. Similarly, most automated purchase requisitioning systems provide the internal user with a catalog of suppliers with items that they may purchase in various spend categories. Their supply request is routed for approval, and once the proper approvals are obtained, it goes directly to the selected catalog supplier. Each supplier has obligatory responsibilities under a Master Supply Agreement or a similar contractual arrangement, which lowers business risk substantially.

- **Review of current market conditions.** For the sourcing team to identify opportunities that exist in the market, outside of the relatively limited picture taken from the organization's experience, a thorough analysis of external market conditions must be taken. This is perhaps the most important step in the planning process since, ideally, it will provide critical benchmarks used to identify areas of supply opportunity when compared with our own organization's overall performance. We can examine many significant fundamentals. Here are some that are perhaps the most common:
  - **Competitive positioning.** To what extent does supplier competition exist? Are there many suppliers or very few? Many suppliers would result in robust competition and the opportunity to leverage and improve our overall cost position. Fewer suppliers might lead to a strategy of placing more of our other types of purchases with these suppliers to gain overall financial leverage, depending on the scope of their business. Similarly, we should know who the major buyers are that create market demand and what likely impact they will have on our sourcing strategy.
  - **Cost profiles.** We need to understand the drivers of market pricing and the likely trends in those areas. This will define our supplier negotiation timing strategy: Rising prices might signal longer-term contracts to lock in current pricing; falling prices may lead to a strategy of spot or one-time buying.
  - **Risk.** Identify significant market and/or political risks affecting our key purchases and develop a strategy to deal with them. We also want to determine how this type of risk will impact our inventory goal positions. Do we need more or less safety stock or alter our lead times?
  - **Supply chain.** For critical items and categories, we want to understand the extent that factors in our extended supply chain will impact our key critical path suppliers. Depending on the length of the

supply chain, transportation and logistics costs can be an area for
further negotiation as well as continued monitoring and analysis.

- **Technological trends.** We need to understand how rapidly the technology changes in major sourcing categories so we can determine
  areas that are due for an engineering turnover or retooling.
- **Financial profiles.** As part of our market review, we should not
  overlook an analysis of the financial position of our suppliers. This
  means looking at market trends in profitability, accounts receivable
  aging, accounts payable aging, cash flow and short-term obligations,
  and comparing our suppliers to the trends in their market segment.

Operational Sourcing Strategy

Strategic sourcing, as a plan, must be implemented—that is, set in
motion—through operational executed activities. A practical way to guide
this process is to develop an implementation initiative. This initiative outlines
those specific operational activities that will support the strategic sourcing
plan. By operational activities, we mean those day-to-day functions common
to most procurement organizations: issuing purchase orders, ordering or
releasing direct materials to plan, forecasting volumes, monitoring supplier
performance, tracking spending patterns, assessing supply risk, resolving
contractual issues, arranging the return of unused product, and reconciling
supplier invoices.

Having an operational plan in place will help to significantly reduce (or
even eliminate) the common tactical fire-drill approach to acquisition.

Steps to Implementing the Plan

The strategic sourcing plan is useful in guiding operational tactics without
actually defining them. But there are some important details that should be
identified when developing an operational sourcing strategy:

- **Current conditions.** For each of the stated strategic objectives, the
  authoring team needs to examine existing conditions and describe them
  in enough detail so that they are easily understood. If the "as-is" situation is not described in the SWOT analysis, this may indicate a need
  to conduct research. For example: The organization needs a 20 percent reduction in procurement governed spending. This is one of the
  strategic plan's objectives. However, it is quickly discovered that three
  primary suppliers are operating at a loss (and unable to provide further discounts) and other potential low-cost suppliers lack capacity

to handle additional volume. Think about how you might handle this situation.

- **Gap analysis.** Current conditions and our stated objectives are obviously *not* in alignment in the example provided. There is a gap between our needs and the situation in the market. We need to identify this gap in specific terms. For example: What percentage of our total spending do these suppliers account for? If it's 10 percent of our total spending of $70 million, we have lost an opportunity to meet the organization's objectives by $1.4 million:

10% of $70 million = $7 million in spending × 20% required savings

= $1.4 million

- **Plan to bridge the gap.** Are any price concessions available? Can we find another way, outside of additional discounts, to narrow the gap? Since our primary suppliers are suffering, could we offer an expedited payment arrangement in exchange for some measure of price discount? That is one approach popularized during economic recessions.

We can also look at areas where cost avoidance is possible. A typical method might be to make up the gap in other areas of spending, perhaps reducing travel expenses by conducting online meetings. And there may be other potential solutions. The point is that we must include the intended areas of savings or cost avoidance in our plan.

If our spending profile looks like that in Figure 1.2, where else would you suggest looking for savings? (Hint: Where is the most likely spending that is not currently managed by our procurement group? Could we effect further cost reductions by capturing this spending?)

Figure 1.2 shows a hypothetical breakdown of organizational spending, divided into four categories.

Operational Objectives

Generally, we implement operational objectives through the use of tactics. What we mean by "tactics" is employing the *appropriate means available* to meet the goals defined in our sourcing strategy. For example, if an organization's long-term strategy is to gain market share through aggressive price competition, its sourcing strategy would likely include robust competition throughout the supply base. In terms of tactics, we would require that each purchase be competed primarily on price (although other factors must be present as well) and that some relinquishment of longer-term supplier relations would be acceptable as a natural outcome.

From a tactical perspective, we can achieve our supply objectives through a number of key operational activities. These activities should align with our strategic objectives as we have defined them in the strategic sourcing plan. The section that follows briefly examines some of the most common operational objectives to be considered.

ENSURE SUPPLY   One of the first considerations in operational supply management activities is to ensure that the necessary goods and services are available when needed. Any number of events can jeopardize the smooth flow of goods and services. To this extent, procurement personnel must continually monitor the working status of requirements within the supply base. Naturally, it would be impossible to monitor the status of each and every order placed, at least with current technology, so close monitoring would apply only to critical items.

What makes an acquisition critical? We can point to a number of factors:

- **Items that directly support the organization's primary business.** These include raw materials, production supplies, energy, and outsourced services. Without these, the organization would not be able to function in its market.
- **Items that are tailored to the organization's specific requirements.** Such items include special tooling and parts, customized software, components of customers' special orders, and specialized employee benefit plans.
- **Items that cannot be substituted.** These are generally materials and services that cannot be produced by another party due to specialized labor, equipment, or patents. Essentially, these are sole-sourced items; that is, only one supplier can provide the product or service.
- **Items whose demand is difficult to forecast.** To meet highly variable demand, we need to be able to forecast usage within the supplier's lead time for production. If we cannot provide accurate forecasts, we must supplement our requirements through safety stock or with other hedging methods.

Ensuring supply also works hand in hand with supply risk assessment (which we go into in the next section). We must enable enough flexibility in our operations to recover from geopolitical events, natural disasters (force majeure), catastrophic events, acts of terrorism, and other unanticipated failures within our supply base. As you will discover, compensating for these circumstances often becomes impossible, so what is really needed is an early assessment and an operational strategy that can accept only a specific level of risk.

IMPROVE VALUE Organizations today are beginning to turn away from simply finding the lowest price and are looking more carefully at how the entire spectrum of value plays out. Best value includes the traditional concept of Total Cost of Ownership (TCOO), in which the entire product life cycle cost is considered, but expands the concept to supply intangibles as well. Using best value means we also measure on-time delivery, quality levels, risk factors, supplier innovation, technology, and service (and flexibility) along with TCOO.

Employing a best value concept does not negate other cost-saving approaches. One of the most common tactics is to consolidate spending and leverage it to effect price reduction. This is a recognized and legitimate way to gain additional value. To do this, we must assemble data on our total volumes (and how they compare with other buying organizations), historical price changes (understanding supplier costs and margins), along with operational improvements initiated by the supplier. We must then decide if our contract terms are adequate, if we are properly positioned to leverage our volume, and where we stand in relation to our competitors. Measuring supply value is not an easy task.

REDUCE SUPPLY RISK Managing supply risk is a complex operational business activity that until recently has been largely ignored in sourcing and procurement. In reality, it is a major factor in supplier selection and thus an integral part of sourcing activities.

Risk reduction has a number of specific features, beginning with identification of potential risks and methods to mitigate them or to develop contingency plans in proportion to the potential severity of the consequences of the risk event. For the most part, sourcing strategy must set limits on the level of risk within the organization's acceptable operational range. Operational strategy calls for constant monitoring and reassessment of risk levels as well as continuous scanning in critical areas for new threats.

From a strategic sourcing perspective, assessing and managing risk is an activity that derives from market and geopolitical research along with other supplier selection methods. We examine this topic in later chapters and expand the concepts into actionable elements.

COORDINATE SUPPLIER ACTIVITIES Although coordinating supplier activities is not a complex process, it is often overlooked in sourcing and procurement activities. Coordinating the activities of suppliers requires an effective planning group and relatively accurate forecasts that are updated in a timely manner. It also requires specific metrics to define the supplier's commitment. We use the term "metrics" in a number of different ways, but in this context we are referring to most common service levels, such as on-time delivery, quality levels, and price reductions. We should also monitor supplier communications with our cross-functional internal users so we understand any issues that arise and can take relatively quick action to resolve them.

ADMINISTER CONTRACT COMPLIANCE   Once a supplier contract is signed, it often gets filed and never looked at again. What a mistake! Contracts must be properly administered to ensure that the supply organization achieves its part of the bargain. Typically, this task goes to the internal user who, more often than not, is far too busy to monitor contract compliance in all but the most strategic areas. The sourcing group, teaming with the end-user and other stakeholders, must establish a contractual Service Level Agreement (SLA) that sets forth the key metrics that the supplier is required to meet over time. Procurement or contract administration groups must then administer the contract by monitoring the supplier's performance to the metrics established. If we are paying for two-week delivery from the time the order is placed, for example, why would we accept delivery in three weeks on a regular basis? If three weeks is fine with the internal users, that's what we should have contracted for and possibly paid less.

Cosourcing

Cosourcing is another aspect of strategic sourcing that plays an increasingly important role in sourcing and procurement activities. The term refers to a service that is performed jointly by internal staff and suppliers. For example, in software development, the using organization might provide the subject matter expertise and develop the requirements, while third parties would develop the architecture and supply the software coding. The benefits of using this approach include the availability of external staff for project work, use of technical expertise that is unavailable in-house, and gaining access to critical knowledge of the market in which we are sourcing.

Although cosourcing has not been used to any great extent in the past, it appears to be gaining favor as an alternative to full outsourcing models. With cosourcing, the using organization can maintain a greater degree of control and has less risk in the supply fulfillment process. (Chapter 10 covers this topic in more detail.)

Supplier Alliances, Partnerships, and Joint Ventures

Collaboration between the buying organization and its suppliers has numerous strategic and operational benefits for both parties. The buyer gains greater leverage in continuity of supply and the supplier gains a loyal customer. In this section, we examine some of the more formal collaborations between the buying organization and the supplying organization, and how they enable other significant aspects of strategic sourcing.

STRATEGIC ALLIANCES   Strategic alliances are one of the more common forms of formal collaboration. They generally involve some manner of commitment to a long-term relationship between the parties. Participating in this method of collaboration, there is shared risk as well as shared benefits, with both parties working toward improving their common operations. A cornerstone of this approach is the exchange of information. Relying on the supplier's resources and knowledge, Early Supplier Involvement enables the two groups to work together as a team, developing improved processes while reducing risk and cost.

Often this relationship is memorialized through a supplier contract. A Master Supply Agreement, for example, sets forth the conditions under which the two organizations will operate and their mutual roles and responsibilities. There are also processes in which suppliers become "certified" by the buying organization, typically to a given set of standards such as those developed by the International Organization for Standardization (ISO). Suppliers are also certified through the quality assurance organization (or supplier quality engineering) that seeks to determine the compatibility of the quality assessment systems with one another. Certification thus provides the buying organization with some assurance that its acceptance standards can be met by the supplier.

Strong alliances are created by relationships through the interaction of personnel in each of the organizations. It could be that executives meet periodically or engineers work together to solve a current problem, or procurement personnel find ways to share sources or other business methods. Increasingly, organizations are developing ways to integrate elements of their information technology infrastructure from a need for immediate and secure communications.

STRATEGIC PARTNERSHIPS   In many cases, strategic partnerships are not much different from strategic alliances. There is some manner of formal agreement to collaborate, a sharing of risk and benefits, and close professional relationships between personnel from both organizations. However, strategic partnerships often involve some form of cosourcing by the buying organization. This might include engineering or design services, manufacturing, distribution, or the development of a new product to be marketed by one of the partners, to mention just a few. In some cases, an equity investment by one or both parties of the strategic partnership is part of the formal arrangement.

Here is an example from a recent press release that outlines the nature of the strategic partnership formed by two companies: One company handles the marketing while its partner runs the fulfillment service.

> *San Diego, California–based Solar Energy and Efficiency Solutions (SEES, Inc.), a leader in providing optimal solutions and highest return on investment to energy efficiency solutions, is announcing its interest in new and revolutionary inventions, discoveries, and consumer information related to renewable energy products covering Wind, Water, and Solar solutions. SEES, Inc., in partnership with fulfillment giant SCI—Suarez Corporation Industries—are assessing and evaluating new products for distribution through the SEES marketing and SCI fulfillment services.*

> *Source:* World-Wire, "SEES, Inc. Open Doors For Strategic Partnerships with Providers of Leading Edge Innovative Renewable Energy Solutions in B-to-B, B-to-C, and Government Sectors," press release, December 30, 2009, www.world-wire.com/news/0912300001.html.

JOINT VENTURES   A joint venture (JV) is characterized by the legal formation of an entirely new business enterprise. Typically, the JV has a limited and specific objective that, once achieved, results in the closing of the entity. A JV is commonly formed to finance an operation, with all parties participating in providing the capital, defraying start-up costs, and sharing in the risks and benefits. The parties also share in the management of the JV.

JVs range the spectrum of partnerships: creation of a manufacturing operation for a product or products that can be used by both parties, a distribution center for products from both organizations, a shared facility, or a research project. On occasion, a corporation will form a JV with a governmental agency that has the ability to finance the operation through the issuance of a bond. This was the case when Advanced Micro Devices, a Sunnyvale, California semiconductor manufacturer, partnered with the government of Saxony (a German state) to build a manufacturing facility in Dresden, Germany. The cost for the manufacturer to undertake this project alone was prohibitive (estimated at over $10 billion), but the government found benefits in reducing unemployment and thus expanding its tax base.

The Sourcing Process

To conclude our overview of strategic sourcing, let's turn briefly to a generalized view of the sourcing process, both strategic and operational. As noted in the preceding sections of this chapter, strategic sourcing has both planning and operational elements. Now we can put it all together into one relatively linear process map.

As you can see in Figure 1.3, there are four main functions:

1. **Strategic planning.** This is the development and alignment of the strategic sourcing strategy with the overall organizational business strategy.
2. **Research.** This segment covers an analysis of internal requirements, market analysis, and prequalification of potential suppliers. Prequalification means that the supplier meets the sound financial conditions required and is in the business of supplying the products or services with competitive pricing. Prequalification is used primarily to develop a competitive group of supply bidders.
3. **Solicitation.** We refer here to the process of preparing our Request for ____ (RFx), evaluating responses, selecting the supplier, conducting negotiations, and forming a contract.
4. **Contract administration.** This is the ongoing process of monitoring the supplier's performance to the contractual agreement, ensuring compliance, conducting business reviews, and generating metrics for continuous performance improvement.

The process map in Figure 1.3 outlines the steps in a strategic sourcing process.

Summary

In this chapter, we provided a step-by-step overview of the strategic sourcing process. In doing so, we touched upon a number of topics: the mission and vision statement, environmental analysis, SWOT analysis, assumptions, objectives, strategy, and implementation.

We examined the process of operational analysis, and the formation of operational plans and objectives. This section included spending analysis, supplier performance issues, competition, and outsourcing opportunities. We also touched on capturing additional spending and improving internal processes, then outlined the analysis of market conditions.

In the section on operational sourcing strategy, we covered the steps needed to implement the strategic plan and perform a gap analysis. Operational objectives were also noted, including processes such as ensuring supply, improving value, reducing supply risk, coordinating supplier activities, and administering contract compliance.

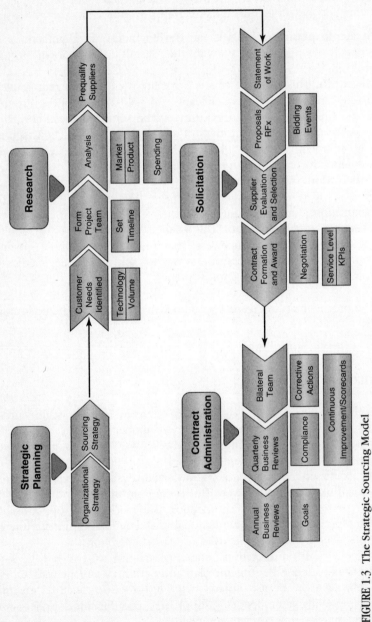

FIGURE 1.3 The Strategic Sourcing Model

Source: Copyright © 2005 eParagon LLC. All rights reserved.

18

We then examined commonly used forms of collaboration between buying organizations and suppliers: cosourcing, strategic alliances, strategic partnerships, and joint ventures. The chapter concluded with an overview of the sourcing process.

Many of these elements are explored in more detail in the coming chapters.

CHAPTER 2

Operational Alignment with Sourcing Strategy

In Chapter 1, we outlined the basic elements of strategic sourcing to provide you with a road map of the entire process. In this chapter, we illustrate how the process actually works by examining the way strategic elements and tactical operational elements come together.

Let's begin with the first step taken in most sourcing actions: understanding the requesting end user's specific requirements. Most of the time, we will be working with high-risk and high-cost commodity elements since they invariably warrant our close attention.

Understanding Requirements

"Requirements" is a term often used in procurement to mean specifications (in the case of materials or products), and the Statement of Work (SOW) for services and customization. Although Statement of Work is technically somewhat different from its closely related term, Scope of Work, the two terms are most commonly used interchangeably.

The SOW has five very important functions.

1. It provides service contractors with a clear set of expectations and important operational guidelines. A good SOW clearly outlines "outcomes" (what we want to achieve) and/or methods through which we expect to achieve completion. SOWs review our objectives, limitations, and the measures used to determine successful acceptance of work completion.
2. It provides the basis upon which the pricing is established and payment made, usually at predetermined milestones or at completion of the work performed.

3. It enables the formation of appropriate contract language that forms the agreement between the buyer and supplier.
4. It clarifies the responsibilities of both parties so that each is prepared to conduct business activities accordingly.
5. It outlines the timeline for completion of the work and provides our internal stakeholders with a basis for coordinating related activities.

Traditionally, the SOW is prepared by the using group, but in many organizations the using group only provides the technical requirements. This leaves most of the other elements (which we examine in a later section) to be developed by the sourcing group.

Here's an example of the technical requirements included in a SOW for emergency call centers developed by one of the U.S. governmental agencies (numbers and names intentionally deleted).

Specific Task Requirements

The contractor shall provide and maintain turnkey service of telephone representatives, Automated Data Processing (ADP) and telecom equipment and network services, including call processing equipment, and facilities and network services for the purpose of responding to incoming calls and accepting applications for disaster assistance. All facilities provided shall conform to the requirements set forth in Section C.5 of the base contract and must be located within the contiguous 48 states.

A minimum of xxxx workstations and xxxx agents is required within 14 days of contract award. The Government requests that the contractor provide staffing up to xxxx maximum within the following 14 days. The work to be performed may be distributed to no more than 6 contact centers. Each center shall have a minimum capacity of xxx agent workstations. All contact center staff will be located at the contractor's facilities.

Services Required

The contractor shall provide the services identified in this section. These services are to be provided in the manner described in Section C.3 of the base contract and this task order SOW.

- Responding to inbound calls and accepting applications for disaster assistance. Only English calls will be routed to the Contractor for response under this task.
- Telecommunications Services

The contractor shall provide all technical and management services to support the task, including program management, technology management, information and relationship management, human resources management, performance management, quality assurance/quality improvement, management reports, security, contingency/disaster recovery, and value engineering.

The contractor shall have call center(s) fully-operational and fully-staffed with a minimum of xxxx phone agents trained with the Government's curriculum within 14 days of issuance of the task order.

The contractor shall ensure that a minimum of xxxx agents are trained and available to answer calls within 48 hours from the time XYZ Agency verifies network and call connectivity.

The Contractor shall adjust within 24 hours of notification

- Staffing
- Schedules and/or
- Hours of Operation

as requested by the government to meet anticipated call volume. The contractor shall maintain a fully-operational facility during the entire term of the task order.

As you can see, this requirements section contains a number of measurable tasks, such as "within 14 days of contract award" and "to no more than 6 contact centers." We also find the statement: "The contractor shall provide all technical and management services to support the task" and a list of the functions to be included. In other words, this is a statement of *what* is to be done, not *how* the work is to be performed. The execution of the stated responsibilities appears to be left in the hands of the contractor.

But then this section follows:

Proposed Work Flow

The Caller dials a toll-free number that is provided by XYZ Agency to seek disaster assistance. The call terminates at an interactive voice response service provided by XYZ Agency. If the caller elects to speak to a Customer Service Representative (CSR), XYZ Agency will make a determination as to how the call should be routed. If XYZ Agency determines that the call should be routed to a contractor-operated center for response, the call will be directed to the contractor system for handling. Calls forwarded for live assistance are queued for handling by a qualified CSR.

> After the caller is routed to a CSR, the CSR responds to the caller's initial request and any other additional requests the caller makes. If the caller desires to register for disaster assistance, the CSR accesses an XYZ Agency disaster assistance registration database via the Intranet or Internet (to be determined by XYZ Agency), probes the caller for specific information, and records the required information needed to complete the registration process. The average time needed to complete the registration process for each caller is estimated to be 20 minutes. An on-line version of the XYZ Agency disaster assistance registration database can be viewed at the XYZ Agency's web site at (URL to be provided).

This section appears to be very prescriptive, telling the contractor exactly how the call center work is to be performed. Do the two sections work together? Or do they conflict? Is one method more correct than another?

These questions bring up the manner in which specifications are addressed in the SOW. For the most part, they are addressed in one of two ways: performance-based specifications or design specifications.

Performance-Based Specifications versus Design Specifications

As we noted, technical requirements are generally provided to the contractor or supplier in the form of a specification. The two most widely used types of specifications are design specifications and performance specifications.

DESIGN SPECIFICATIONS A design specification outlines exactly how we want the contractor to perform the service or by what method the supplier must make the product. Design specifications leave no room for innovation and typically contain an implied warranty that the contractor can produce the desired results if the specification is followed precisely. If the outcome is not as expected, it is the fault of the specification, not the contractor. Thus, the full risk is on the shoulders of the purchaser.

PERFORMANCE SPECIFICATIONS Performance specifications focus on outcomes or results rather than how to achieve them. They enable the contractor to use its expertise and innovation to produce the desired results. Instead of detailing the methods to be used, the performance specification details the required outcomes in specific and measurable terms. Industry-specific standards are often referenced that need to be adhered to in fulfilling the performance outcome. These measures or metrics are included in the SOW, often as part of a Service Level Agreement (SLA), and are stated in the absolute terms of Key Performance Indicators (KPIs). There is no warranty for a performance specification since the methods to be used to produce the desired results are chosen by the contractor. In this case, the risk is shared by both contractor and purchaser.

CHOOSING THE TYPE OF SPECIFICATION The type of specification used depends on factors such as technical knowledge (which party has the domain expertise) and the amount of flexibility we have to employ various supply fulfillment solutions. There is really no hard-and-fast rule, however, and we often find organizations using hybrid versions that combine elements of both types of specifications. In the two examples provided, the first section is very much a performance specification while the second example is a design specification.

Typical Elements of a Statement of Work

Before we examine the role that planning, both strategic and operational, holds in developing the SOW, let's further examine some of the elements that are commonly found in SOWs.

DELIVERABLES AND PERFORMANCE We must identify the criteria by which we will determine that the work has been completed satisfactorily. Often this is referred to as acceptance criteria, which, when signed off by the responsible using group, becomes the basis for issuing final acceptance and payment. We may also want to outline the KPIs that need to be followed during the course of the contract. Each KPI should state how and by whom they are to be measured and reported. Here is how it might look using our previous example.

Performance Standard

The contractor should adhere to Citizen Customer Service Level (CSLIC)–recommended standards for contact centers, whenever applicable. High-level standards include: (1) Respond by email within two business days to 90% of emails received; (2) Give callers an estimate of phone wait time after 30 seconds on hold; (3) Answer letters or estimate response time within 15 days of receiving original inquiry; and (4) Keep citizen wait on walk-in service to 15 minutes. The contractor should review and adhere to the recommendations in the CSLIC report entitled "Proposed Performance Measures, Practices and Approaches for Government-wide Customer Contact Activities" and the supporting documentation by MITRE on the USA Services web site.

Deliverables are often summarized in the form of a Work Breakdown Structure (WBS) that lists them in abbreviated task format. The WBS enables

TABLE 2.1 Work Breakdown Structure

Task	Deliverable	Due Date	Acceptance
1.10	Select all sites for Contact Centers	05/16/xx	Approval by _____
2.10	Build out _____ workstations	06/16/xx	Per standard xyz
3.10	Select and install telephone system	06/30/xx	Per standard uvw
4.10	Hire _____ agents	07/15/xx	Meet Qual # 123

easy tracking and communication. It can also be used to establish milestones in a project management environment.

Table 2.1 is a simplified version of how the WBS might look.

SCHEDULE The SOW needs to specify when each of the deliverables is due for completion. It is important to use realistic dates so that dependent activities (such as installation, in the case of customized equipment) can be properly scheduled. As noted earlier, dates are used in a project management environment to establish milestones.

SERVICE LEVEL AGREEMENT An SLA states the measurements that the contractor will be obligated to meet. The SLA can be included as a separate section of the SOW or simply included as metrics in each section requiring a performance standard. It can also be included as an addendum to the SOW. For contract administration or performance monitoring, it is probably wise to create it as a separate document for the sake of the convenience of having all metrics in one place.

REGULATORY REQUIREMENTS This section describes any known legal or regulatory requirements that the contractor is required to follow in the performance of the work. Examples would include any special hazardous material handling procedures, specialized certifications for personnel performing specific duties, and licensing requirements. It is not uncommon, however, to find clauses in the actual contract covering this requirement since it is often considered an adjunct to liability limitations. Services procurements are typically governed by common law while tangible goods procurements are governed by the Uniform Commercial Code (UCC).

INTELLECTUAL MATERIAL The SOW must include the assignment of responsibility for the development of any significant intellectual property or proprietary processes. This assignment usually results in language included in the contract specifying ownership title of specific work product methods. From the example SOW provided earlier, is it clear who develops the material and who owns it?

REPORTING AND COMMUNICATIONS   Reporting requirements are an important part of the SOW. It is necessary for the contractor or services supplier to account for required reports in its pricing structure; we don't want to be obliged to create a separate document or order later and have to negotiate pricing separately.

There are a number of reporting formats, and their contents typically depend on the nature of the product or service being reported on. We commonly ask for weekly or monthly status reports on progress so we can be alerted to any incomplete or late items. It is advisable to have performance reports outlining the contractor's assessment of metrics with expected completion dates. We also want assessment reports to include corrective action reports to ensure satisfactory remedies to any shortfalls. In addition, it is helpful to have the supplier submit a list of open invoices (an aging report) so that we can compare it to the reports created by our organization's accounting group.

PERSONNEL: SPECIAL QUALIFICATIONS   It is not unusual for the SOW to include any special personnel requirements necessary. It may include special training that we feel is important as well as licensing and professional certification or individual experience levels. Including this requirement ensures that we get the right personnel where they are needed. If we want specifically named individuals in positions, such as a particular project manager, it is more appropriate to include this in a clause within the terms of the contract rather than the SOW.

How the SOW Links to Strategic Planning

Once the SOW has been analyzed and understood to the extent needed to use it in a supply solicitation (such as a Request for Proposal), we can link the sourcing effort to both strategic and tactical operational plans. Since guidelines differ from organization to organization, we will attempt to point out only generalized linkages.

ALLIANCE AND PARTNERSHIP STRATEGIES   If our strategy calls for engaging previously used suppliers with whom we have formed special relationships, our first step prior to issuing any formal, public solicitation will be to review historical contracts that may include similar requirements. Doing this will establish whether we have used any of our preferred suppliers for similar work. If we have, we may be in a position to ask those suppliers to review the current SOW and prepare scope and/or methods comments or recommendations. Our objectives are:

1. We will reinforce our existing supplier relationships by providing an Early Supplier Involvement (ESI) opportunity for preferred suppliers to win the work.
2. By using an existing supplier(s), we will substantially shorten the sourcing cycle, eliminating the need for market research and supplier qualification. Doing so will likely simplify the overall bidding and contracting process and prove an advantage to the using group.

However, using an existing supplier will not relieve us of the responsibility of negotiating favorable terms and conditions or pricing.

COMPETITIVE BIDDING STRATEGIES   If our strategy calls for competitively bidding each major acquisition, however, we will proceed on another tack. We will need to prepare for supply solicitation (examined in Chapter 6) by conducting a review of the market (and our own historical supply records) to locate potentially qualified suppliers and understand the market conditions that currently drive *their* strategies. We will have to take into account the degree of competition in the market as well as economic trends in order to properly prepare the solicitation strategy.

The competitive bidding process, along with its elements of market research, solicitation, selection criteria, and evaluation, requires additional time to complete. This time, however, should be regarded as an investment in the organization's future that must be used wisely and never rushed.

Opportunity Analysis

Chapter 1 examined the concepts of opportunity analysis in some detail. Our objective in this section is to explain how employing specific operational strategies and tactics are linked to our strategic sourcing objectives. We can do this by examining specific business areas in which to conduct our opportunity analysis.

Spend Analysis

Spend analysis is one of the basic tools in use today to help rationalize our procurement patterns and supplier selections. By the term "rationalize," we mean the process of consolidating suppliers of the same or similar capabilities to drive greater procurement volumes through fewer supply entities. Many organizations buy the same or very similar items or services from several suppliers. Directing more spending through fewer suppliers usually leads to better pricing and reduced costs.

Through consolidation, it is also much easier to cut down on maverick spending (spending outside preferred supplier contracts) and monitor preferred supplier contract compliance to help ensure that the bargained-for savings are actually realized. In addition to cost savings, there are other benefits of a fully functioning spend analysis system: easier contract administration, stronger Supplier Relationship Management (SRM), improved internal communication operations, and better visibility into our overall spending patterns. We can also use spend analysis as a benchmarking tool, comparing our patterns to those found in our industry or to other researched best practices.

One of our authors recalls an incident that occurred in a high-tech company where he was previously employed:

Our VP of Procurement held weekly staff meetings with the group's managers. During one such meeting he suggested we develop a plan to reduce the number of suppliers we used. His take was that we had far too many suppliers.

For the most part this wasn't very high on our radar. We had plenty of initiatives still unfinished. But he doggedly continued. Week after week he would bring up the subject and ask how many suppliers we had eliminated in the past week. No one answered . . . ever.

Then, during one of our meetings, he asked us all to follow him out of the conference room. He took us over to a section of the department that had a long run of cubicles. There, tacked to the outside of the block, was a long stretch of copy paper that appeared to contain a list of some kind. I would guess it ran about 30 feet and was printed in relatively small type.

"Here," he announced, "is the current list of suppliers. There are over 17,000. Count them if you like." Then he just turned and walked away.

We all stood there for a few minutes looking at the list and shaking our heads. Each of us must have had the same idea, because at the following week's meeting, as we went around the table reporting each group's status and progress, every one of us noted how many suppliers we had designated for consolidation.

EMPLOYING SPEND ANALYSIS   To be used effectively, the spend analysis process should begin with a systematic approach to gathering data, not just once but on a continuing basis. Often this analysis requires specialized software to properly aggregate the existing data, although many ERP (Enterprise

Resource Planning, an organization-wide data-processing program) software programs routinely include this capability in their systems. There are also many third-party service providers that will perform the analysis for you on a fixed-fee basis.

Without dedicated software, conducting a spend analysis can be a daunting task, especially when doing it for the first time. Cleansing and classifying data so that it falls into the right commodity categories can be both time consuming and frustrating. You will need to use existing data from your procurement operations or from accounts payable or procurement-card supplier payment records, and attempt to sort the data by line item rather than by general ledger coding. Accounting categories do not necessarily link directly to spending commodity categories.

Even with the proper tools, there will still be items that we have to initially code by hand. In fact, it is possible to conduct a spend analysis manually using data from existing records and importing it into an Excel spreadsheet, manually coding the data by category and then sorting it. Doing this will also enable you to systematically review data that would not fit into its proper category when downloaded from the ERP or legacy system. However, keep in mind that this would not be a repeatable process. We suggest limiting the scope of your analysis to the most important spend categories first, so that you can develop the process in small steps, and it does not greatly disrupt normal business operations.

When spend analysis first became widely marketed, consultants and software providers often pointed to the problems inherent in gathering data: multiple computer systems, decentralized procurement and accounting, and the use of different nomenclature for the same items. Some liked to point out that overall spending data with individual suppliers could be difficult to develop since the same organization was often listed in the supplier register in a number of different ways. The example we recall was that of IBM, or I.B.M., or International Business Machines, or Int'l Bus Mach ... and so on. Is this still a problem in your organization?

As we begin the process of rationalizing categories and reducing suppliers, we will likely discover that some of them are under contract and cannot be eliminated at this particular time. However, we do have the opportunity to consolidate the others and, in the process, negotiate terms that are better than those we have with our existing contracted suppliers. We might find that engaging suppliers by contract might prove beneficial. Or perhaps we may discover that the existing terms we have are better than those offered by others. That's always good information to have.

LINKAGE TO STRATEGIC PLANNING By now, we trust you can recognize how employing spend analysis on an operational level can support your strategic sourcing objectives for cost reduction. Similarly, opportunity analysis receives direction from the broader business operational strategy. Where we look for opportunities depends on what we expect to achieve and the resources available to implement our strategic objectives. Just as we expect the strategic plan for sourcing to link to the organization's strategic plan, we must ensure that the operational tactics we use effectively support our strategic objectives.

LIMITATIONS Therefore, if our goal is to consolidate the supply base in order to lower operating costs, spend analysis can be an extremely useful tool. It is a concept whose effectiveness is well supported by research and benchmark studies and examples. But what if our key strategic sourcing objective is to acquire the latest technology? Would spend analysis directly support this? Likely not. What if we are a manufacturer with far too many component parts that are becoming an increasing burden on our planners and materials staff; can spend analysis help us standardize and reduce the number of parts we are required to support? Certainly not; spend analysis is primarily an engineering function, albeit supported by the sourcing team. So we need to develop a number of operational approaches to achieving objectives.

Other Cost Reduction Processes

There are a number of other opportunities for the sourcing team to support the strategic plan through cost reduction, in addition to rationalizing the supply base and consolidating spend categories. We can generally discover them through the opportunity analysis we described earlier. In the next sections, we briefly examine those commonly used in sourcing operations.

OUTSOURCING We generally define outsourcing as the process of moving operational functions performed internally that are not considered core competencies to a third-party supplier. This is usually done to reduce cost, but often it is a way to leverage the domain expertise of a third party for more effective operations or to gain access to newer technology that specialist organizations already have in place.

The Buy American provision in the American Recovery and Reinvestment Act of 2009 (Section 1605 of Title XVI) states that none of the funds may be used for the construction, alteration, or repair of a public building or public work unless all the iron, steel, and manufactured goods used are produced in the United States. In an April 2009 survey by CBS News/*New York Times*, 66 percent of the respondents said that "trade with other countries—both buying and selling products" is good for the U.S. economy.

Today, outsourcing has a global marketplace, and our processes can be sourced anywhere in the world. Some of the commonly outsourced functions include logistics, accounting (especially payroll and accounts payable), design, engineering, human resources, information technology, customer support call centers, fulfillment, travel services and, occasionally, research and development or manufacturing. We examine the entire outsourcing process in more detail in Chapter 12.

COMMODITY MANAGEMENT The reference to "commodities" (sometimes called categories) in sourcing and procurement operations does not always mean those commodities that are traded on a public exchange, such as the Chicago Mercantile Exchange. Many organizations group their procurement teams by the industries or categories of services that they manage (e.g., chemicals, computer hardware, office supplies, etc.). This specialization enables us to employ professionals who understand the operation of the category industries they manage and can better support the organization's sourcing needs. Some of the benefits from this strategy include:

- **Leveraging price cycles.** Prices for many items we source follow cyclical business trends of one form or another. Some prices go up and down based on seasonal demand factors; others follow macro- or microeconomic cycles. It is difficult for those not familiar with the particular category or commodity to understand these types of cycles and therefore leverage them. Tactically, we want to source, purchase, or contract when prices are at (or close to) their low point. Since prices are essentially driven by supply and demand, and can often become volatile, the timing of our purchases is critical. A category or commodity expert is better positioned to understand the nature of these market cycles and, as a result, better time the purchases or supply contracts to take advantage of cyclically of lower prices.
- **Standardization.** Often organizations acquire goods dedicated to a particular need. When a similar need arises at a later time, the existing items are overlooked and new goods are specified. Sometimes there are just minor differences between them. Over time, it is not unusual for an organization to have many redundant goods. Just as we find an opportunity to reduce prices through consolidating suppliers, consolidating goods can produce similar benefits. The same principle of greater volumes equaling lower prices applies. For this reason, forming a team with our category or commodity group, sourcing group, engineering group, and the user group to evaluate redundant goods can produce dividends.

A small furniture manufacturer we know installed a computerized Bill of Material and discovered it was using 56 different sizes of screws across its operation. After its engineer had time to consider a consolidation, the number was reduced to just 8.

MATERIAL SUBSTITUTIONS Systematizing an opportunity analysis to look for alternative materials can produce excellent results. Although specifying materials is an engineering or design function, sourcing and procurement have greater access to suppliers and are more likely to discover less expensive materials that can replace those already in use. For example, using a generic brand with the exact specifications of its branded counterpart will most often produce lower prices.

There are also conditions under which one material can be substituted for another, providing the replacement material can deliver the same specifications and functional performance at a lower price. As an example, when copper prices escalated recently, some users switched to polyethylene tube as a suitable substitute in plumbing applications.

Here is an interesting example of a successful material substitution that produced multiple benefits:

Environmentally Driven Substitution

At an operation in Brazil, granulation and coating of a proprietary product used significant amounts of harmful chemicals, including methylene chloride, an ingredient with a highly toxic profile. Methylene chloride also accounted for a very large portion of the organization's toxic emissions.

Engineers tested several alternatives and after a two-year evaluation, either replaced the methylene chloride with a nontoxic material or eliminated it altogether for each step.

REVERSE AUCTIONS The use of reverse auctions was popularized in the late 1990s. The concept of a reverse auction is relatively simple: Invite suppliers to a "live" online competitive bidding event where they vie for a specific segment of the organization's business. Suppliers can view competitors' bids as they are placed (but the names are never revealed) and can respond accordingly. Typically, reverse auctions are hosted by a neutral third party responsible for ensuring that participants know how to use the process and that the auction is conducted fairly.

Hosts for the reverse auction activity boasted as much as a 35 percent savings using this process, and, in fact, one of our authors experienced reductions significantly better than that at a major U.S. corporation. Keep in mind, however, that many of these reductions occurred during a time of recession, when prices were already declining. It is much more difficult to achieve significant savings during a time of increasing prices.

INVENTORY REDUCTION   Although it does not necessarily provide a direct cost savings, inventory reduction can free up financial resources that are tied up in stocked items. The advent of computerized MRP (Material Requirements Planning) provided demand and forecast visibility for components used in manufacturing operations and helped better manage inventory practices. Algorithms were developed early on to help ensure an adequate flow of materials within the parameters of a closely monitored manufacturing system.

JUST IN TIME   Using the capability of MRP, the Just-in-Time (JIT) or "lean" process has been extensively popularized since the 1950s. Inventory, according to JIT philosophy, is waste. JIT and its associated concepts of waste reduction and rapid throughput is probably the most revolutionary change in manufacturing methods since the advent of the production line and a specialized labor force. In fact, many attribute the practice to Henry Ford and the first use of automated "mass production" manufacturing techniques.

It is obvious to see how JIT requires strong supplier relationships. Stock outages can shut down entire production lines, so it is critical to select suppliers whose systems can support rapid fulfillment of demand-generated orders. As a supplier selection process that grows out of a strategic plan calling for the implementation of inventory and waste reduction, rapid fulfillment becomes a key operational sourcing activity.

CONSIGNMENT   To further support aggressive inventory management, companies often rely on the process of supplier-consigned inventory. Using this method, suppliers stock required materials right at the organization's production facility so that it is available exactly when needed. Materials are not paid for until they are actually withdrawn from storage. The benefit to suppliers in most cases is that the withdrawal creates an electronic invoice (and more rapid payment) so that the supplier can reduce its administrative cost. It also provides what amounts to a franchise, a lock on the business, since the system invariably requires single sourcing.

Using consignment inventory requires the buying organization to provide both a forecast of demand and a guarantee to purchase a specified amount of inventory should the material become obsolete. Ultimately, though, it is hard to see how consignment inventory actually reduces waste. If holding inventory is undesirable for the buying organization, how is it any better for the supplier?

Reduced inventory levels and JIT techniques are most commonly implemented through both short-term and long-term category management objectives (discussed in the next section) that emerge from operational strategy. They are thus closely supported by the sourcing team. As we discuss in later chapters covering market research and source selection, it is critical to have high-level management support for implementing this inventory reduction strategy. Users have a tendency to operate under a "just-in-case" hoarding of supplies.

REENGINEERING WITH VALUE ANALYSIS   Value analysis is a systematic process used in the design or redesign of products and services that is based on providing all the necessary functions at the most economic cost within the required level of quality and performance. The process employs techniques that identify all of the required functions and characteristics of an item and establishes values for each of them, arriving at the lowest overall cost within the scope of its required performance. Value analysis, therefore, links cost and function.

Two employees at the General Electric Company during World War II, Lawrence Miles and Harry Erlicher, are credited with creating value analysis. The system almost immediately became a critical part of manufacturing. Because of the war, there were always shortages of materials and component parts. By utilizing value analysis, Miles and Erlicher continually looked for acceptable substitutes for items that were in scarce supply. They found that these substitutions frequently reduced costs or improved the product, or both. What originated from critical necessity turned into a systematic process that they named value analysis.

Looking at it another way, value analysis is a tool for analyzing the value of any specific element's function in relation to its cost, eliminating those elements that add cost without adding corresponding value. For example, it may be possible to eliminate certain expensive housing materials for a machine by improving the shipping container at a lower cost.

Category Segmentation

So far we have considered sourcing strategies and operational methods in generalized terms, as they could apply to any organization. But in actuality, how would you strategically group sourcing and procurement activities so that they can be managed cohesively by a single team? To help answer this question, we can look at some typical examples.

Direct Materials

Direct materials, as the name implies, are those parts and components that go directly into the product sold to the using customer. The nature of the organization's products determines the type of parts and components that go into the manufacturing operations, so they may be grouped differently in different industries. However, here we show how we believe they should be organized based on the nature of the markets and the similarity of the expertise required:

- Raw materials: metals
- Raw materials: chemicals, plastics, gases
- Electronic components
- Fabricated metals
- Fabricated plastics
- Packaging
- Nonmetallic mineral products
- Textiles and fabrics
- Lumber and wood products
- Outsourced manufacturing operations

Indirect Materials and Services

Indirect materials and services are the products and services that do not go directly into the product but rather support the organization's overall operations. Some typical categories:

- Facilities management, including janitorial, landscaping, furniture, energy, and security
- Travel management, including airfare, hotels, car rentals, and relocation services
- Information technology, including software, hardware, network services, and telecommunications
- Purchasing cards
- Office supplies and copy services
- Vehicles and fleet management
- Advertising and marketing services, including printing, media, and promotional material
- Business consulting, engineering, and legal services, including insurance, education, and training
- Capital equipment, for manufacturing and nonmanufacturing

- Outsourced operations, including call center, distribution, accounting, human resources, logistical services, and security
- Logistics, including shipping and transportation

Summary

In this chapter we covered the operational alignment necessary to implement a strategic sourcing plan. This included the process of understanding the end user's requirements and analyzing the Statement of Work as well as understanding the difference between performance-based and design specifications (and how to choose between them). We also covered the elements of an SOW: deliverables and performance, schedule, Service Level Agreements, regulatory requirements, intellectual material, reporting and communications, and the requirement for named personnel or personnel with specific qualifications. The section ended with a discussion of how the SOW links to strategic planning, including alliance and partnership strategies and competitive bidding strategies.

Then we examined spend analysis, supply base rationalization, and other cost reduction processes. We discussed outsourcing, commodity/category management, standardization, material substitutions, reverse auctions, inventory reduction processes, and value analysis.

We concluded the chapter with an outline of broad commodity or category segmentation using direct as well as indirect commodities or categories.

CHAPTER 3

Source to Settle (S2S)

P rocurement sourcing concepts have changed significantly over recent decades. Where we used to see the procurement (or purchasing) function as a stand-alone process—isolated, as it were—to essentially transactional activities such as issuing purchase orders and expediting deliveries, we now see the overall function as consisting of multiple interconnected services. Today, many organizations view this expanded concept of procurement as a start-to-finish process that begins with supplier sourcing activities and concludes when the supplier is paid.

Forward-thinking organizations are adopting a Source-to-Settle (S2S) strategy that integrates sourcing, procurement, and accounts payable. Typically, this integration occurs through an Enterprise Application Software (EAS) application (such as SAP) or Business Process Outsourcing (BPO), but as a discipline, the concept can be implemented in almost any automated business process environment. Figure 3.1 shows the evolution of S2S.

Why Source to Settle?

There are a number of compelling benefits to employing an S2S operational strategy. As an integrated process, S2S enables an agile approach to fulfilling customer demand, and moves the organization toward the full scope of managing the entire supply chain effectively.

Issues

If you carefully examine the acquisition processes of most organizations, you will likely find that they are highly fragmented and decentralized. Often the supply sourcing function is controlled by the end user; geographically dispersed organizations conduct sourcing and procurement operations independent of one another. Spend data are often nonexistent; when such

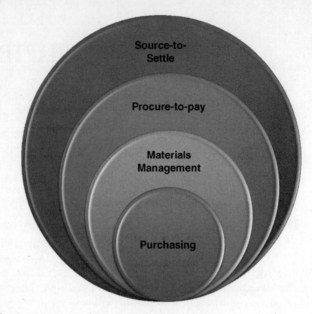

FIGURE 3.1 The Evolution of Source to Settle

data exist, often they are inaccurate due to the lack of quality in the data-gathering process. This fragmentation leads to costly inconsistencies, such as implementing multiple sourcing strategies across the organization and encouraging redundant activities.

LACK OF UNIFORM PROCESSES In this fragmented environment, there is little or no automation in the data collection process. Reliance on manual processes and paperwork thus adds unnecessary cost and mistakes to operations. Manual processes decrease operational visibility in supplier selection and spending patterns; the information that is available is often spotty and untimely. Without a centralized approach to contracting, compliance is generally not encouraged or, when it is, not effectively carried out, so we can expect to find multiple suppliers for the same products or services. We can also expect to find that approvals often occur after the actual purchase (maverick spending).

LACK OF COMPLIANCE It is easy to understand how a fragmented environment makes auditing and compliance monitoring difficult. So-called maverick spending, which refers to purchasing actions outside existing contracts or from nonpreferred suppliers, plagues many organizations since it does not leverage the preferential cost benefits of buying through approved sources.

Lack of compliance extends beyond just off-contract spending. In fact, many organizations have a host of procurement policies that are not being followed:

- **Approval work flow.** Most organizations have a policy that requires some form of approval for virtually all products and services purchased by the organization. Although this is sometimes a blanket approval (as in the case of direct materials used in manufacturing), approval is typically required for any other purchase. Circumventing the required approval work flow by using expense accounts, for example, is a frequently cited occurrence that hinders the process of consolidating purchases to improve pricing. In a publicly held company, this form of circumvention can lead to unreported obligations as outlined under the Sarbanes-Oxley Act (SOX) if the problem is significant enough. Many organizations use the Enterprise Risk Management (ERM) process developed by COSO (Committee of Sponsoring Organizations of the Treadway Commission). This ERM process provides a framework for risk management that emphasizes the importance of identifying and managing risks across the enterprise.
- **Conflict of interest.** Following conflict-of-interest guidelines as a Code of Conduct is another procurement policy that is extremely important to the organization's health. A conflict of interest occurs in any situation where the individual puts his or her personal interests ahead of the organization's needs. Favoring one supplier over another as a result of perks or favors provided, such as meals or tickets to a football game, becomes a conflict of interest, if not in actuality, certainly in the perception of others.

The Consequences of Foul Play

A former corporate buyer and a former vice president (VP) for a subcontractor pled guilty to conspiracy, violating the anti-kickback statute, mail fraud, money laundering, and federal income tax fraud. The VP also pled guilty to engaging in a racketeering enterprise.

The subcontractor's VP paid the buyer kickbacks; in exchange, the buyer agreed to steer business from his company to a wholly owned subsidiary of the subcontractor. The buyer then directed approximately $6 million in repair contracts from his company to the subcontractor's subsidiary and was paid approximately $100,000 in kickbacks.

- **Open competition.** When was the last time a high-value product or service was opened for competitive bids: three years ago, five years ago? Many organizations, especially those in the public procurement sector, require competitive bidding to ensure they are receiving prices and terms that are current in their industries.

Compliance is considered a major issue in government as well. The Department of Defense, for example, has an entire organization dedicated to ensuring full contract compliance called the Defense Contract Management Agency (DCMA). According to a statement on its web site, the agency "monitors contractors' performance and management systems to ensure that cost, product performance, and delivery schedules are in compliance with the terms and conditions of the contracts." This is a rather unique role for any governmental agency; it not only manages performance but the systems used to ensure it. Thus DCMA also monitors the competitive bidding *process* to ensure that taxpayers' money is spent as frugally as possible.

Objectives and Benefits of an S2S Process

In addition to resolving the issues just noted, the S2S system enables organizations to achieve a number of other objectives. Many of these are broad objectives that flow from the organization's overall strategic plan, while others can be considered purely operational. We examine the most important of these objectives next.

COST REDUCTION/COST AVOIDANCE   At the heart of any for-profit business strategy is the need to operate profitably. Doing so involves more aspects than the scope of this book covers, but it also clearly refers to reducing the cost of purchased goods and services as well as avoiding any additional cost through wise decision making.

SPEND VISIBILITY   The S2S process focuses on employing automated methods to help analyze the organization's spending patterns and rationalize supplier consolidation or aggregation. Aggregating purchases made from many suppliers to one or two typically results in financial leverage in terms of cost savings. To do this effectively, however, requires clean and reliable data covering historical spending patterns, both in commodity categories and by supplier. This is a difficult requirement; even with the best data collection and reporting system, it has been estimated that only 85 percent of the line items purchased can be properly identified by automated analysis of a given spend category. The rest, if it accounts for any significant spending, must be identified and processed manually.

REGULATORY COMPLIANCE   The Sarbanes-Oxley Act of 2002 requires certain financial controls and reporting as part of a publicly traded corporation's responsibility to its shareholders and the U.S. Securities and Exchange Commission. To meet these obligations, corporations must have in place a systematic procedure to gather the necessary procurement-related information during the S2S process. In addition, SOX mandated a number of reforms to enhance corporate responsibility, enhance financial disclosures, and combat corporate and accounting fraud, and created the Public Company Accounting Oversight Board to oversee the activities of the business process auditing profession.

Within government procurement processes, many regulatory requirements require equally close monitoring. The Federal Acquisition Regulations (FAR) is an extensive compendium of regulations that require compliance and, as anyone familiar with it will tell you, it is an exceptionally complex body of legislation that requires organizations doing business with the federal government to produce rather extensive reports. Without an S2S system in place, these requirements are very difficult to meet.

Anti-Kickback Act of 1986

The Anti-Kickback Act of 1986 . . . was passed to deter subcontractors from making payments and contractors from accepting payments for the purpose of improperly obtaining or rewarding favorable treatment in connection with a prime contract or subcontract relating to a prime contract. The Act—

(a) Prohibits any person from—
    (1) Providing, attempting to provide, or offering to provide a kickback;
    (2) Soliciting, accepting, or attempting to accept any kickback;
    (3) Including, directly or indirectly, the amount of a kickback in the contract price charged by a subcontractor to a prime contractor [and ultimately the government].

Source: FAR 3.502-2.

STANDARDIZED PROCESSES   The Source-to-Settle structure demands repeatable and consistent processes throughout the organization in order to ensure that it can be managed properly. Gaining the maximum advantage of its benefits requires standardization in all key areas of the acquisition process *before* implementation. If we simply convert our faulty manual processes to one that is automated, we will likely create even more chaos than we already have. Areas of particular importance include sourcing methodologies such as market research; electronic requests for proposal, quotation, and so on (eRFxs); online auctions (eAuctions); supplier selection, procurement, and contract administration; Supplier Relationship Management (SRM); supplier performance reporting and improvement; and Accounts Payable or electronic payment.

Specifically, standardization in sourcing requires uniform methods of analysis for assessing suppliers during the qualification, bidding, and selection phase. Doing this calls for establishing a set of metrics to evaluate and qualify suppliers (often referred to as scorecards). These are measures that, if properly chosen, can be used after the supplier is selected for ongoing supplier performance evaluations and reviews.

Other important elements of standardization include formats for eRFxs, eAuctions, requests for proposals, and requests for quotes, along with general terms and conditions for each of the major categories of goods and services. Uniform contracts for Master Supply Agreements and Master Service Agreements (MSAs) would also fit into this standardization category. In short, all elements in the S2S process must be governed by organization-wide policy and procedures, with automated systems and analytical software helping to ensure ongoing compliance.

REDUCED TRANSACTIONAL COST   Automation is the first rule of reducing transactional costs both in procurement and payables. Numerous automated procurement systems are available, and they extend all the way to small businesses. We focus first on the requisitioning process, automating purchase requests through online catalogs created by suppliers with whom we have existing contracts. With an automated system, the user selects the items needed from a consolidated catalog that enables a search for products he or she is eligible to purchase. The request is then routed via automated work flow for approval. Once approved, it can be electronically directed to the supplier via Electronic Data Interchange (EDI) or eXtensible Markup Language (XML) data feeds. The sourcing group's involvement is with the selection of the suppliers and the negotiation of pricing and terms.

We can also automate invoicing using e-commerce technology or EDI, often at very little or no cost, depending on our existing level of automation. For example, an automated accounts payable is easily implemented with installed Enterprise Resource Planning (ERP) or S2S software, such as Oracle, SAP, and a host of others. Recently, XML has become a payment standard that enables the global use of electronic business information in an interoperable, secure, and consistent manner by all trading partners. And of course, using purchasing cards (P-cards) to reduce low-price or one-time purchases has been a standard practice for some time. Both of these methods not only reduce tactical hands-on transactions, but they enhance supplier relations through consistent, on-time payments.

SUPPLIER INTEGRATION   Many S2S systems include a module or section for SRM. This module is designed to provide stronger collaboration with suppliers by increasing the level of integration with your organization. To a large extent, doing this means reducing payment cycles to agreed-on terms through monitoring and cash flow planning, which goes a long way to improve good relations. It also better enables buying organizations to leverage discounts offered for early payment, which often adds up to a substantial annual amount of cost savings.

Effective supplier integration often helps both organizations reduce the cost of transaction processing through readily available electronic methods. At the same time, it can also improve transaction accuracy. Fewer errors improve the quality of operations since less time is required to resolve or rework them.

RISK MANAGEMENT   Lately, supply chain business risk has become a major focal point in organizations. We are recognizing that the success of any program typically depends on events occurring as we planned. But often we find that is just not the case. Delays occur in supplier delivery, products and services are not available when we need them, or the quality of our purchase is not up to agreed-on standards. As a result, costly production delays eat away at our profit, and worse still, we have disappointed customers.

How does the S2S process help organizations meet their overall risk management objectives? A number of S2S monitoring tools are available as of this writing, but keep in mind that financial markets are currently in turmoil and new processes will likely emerge to deal with contemporary situations.

- **Contract exposure.** Contractual obligations, especially financial ones requiring the buyer to pay for a certain amount of goods or services whether used or not, are a significant financial concern and require close monitoring. Consumer spending habits often change rapidly, so work or materials in the pipeline can become obsolete in a very short time. Because of this, dealing with suppliers who have the ability to meet demand quickly, with relatively short lead times, is an absolute necessity to reduce the financial exposure inherent in a long supply chain or in long lead times. This case applies equally to buyer and seller.

An Example of Contract Risk

Toward the end of the dot-com boom, in the summer of 2001, Cisco Systems, a leading computer network company, startled analysts with the announcement that it had its first loss of earnings in more than 10 years. Sales of its products were down by about 30 percent.

As a result, Cisco had to write off inventory, both on hand and committed to purchase, worth a reported $2.2 billion. This write-off occurred despite the sophisticated technology Cisco had in place to monitor economic conditions.

The fault in this example lies not only with poor demand forecasting but with the integration of its entire procurement system. Obviously, the supply-side planners were not provided with the information pointing to a decline in the macroeconomy and a fall-off in customer demand orders. A demand planning system integrated with production planning may have solved the problem to some extent. However, it was just a matter of time before a disaster such as this one occurred without a fully enabled, completely integrated sourcing system that places high value on an agile supply chain. An S2S system that monitors suppliers' lead times and inventory availability against sourcing criteria will likely go a long way toward solving this type of situation.

- **Financial stability.** Large-scale supplier financial failure is a very real possibility, as we have learned recently. In the future, "too big to fail" may no longer become an option. In accounts payable, for example, credit risk can be related to the stability of the buyer's bank or line of credit. A bank closing often means a total disaster for a company's cash flow if its business or its suppliers' businesses are linked directly or indirectly to that financial institution. Credit risk changes very rapidly now, and as we have seen, supplier credit lines can disappear virtually overnight. In the past, systemic risk—where a domino effect of bank closings occurs and affects the entire system—has been managed largely by central banking regulators, but, as we have seen in the recession of 2007 to 2009, temporary interruptions are likely possible. In this case, risk monitoring systems tied to the organization's financial monitoring system will likely become the tool of choice.
- **Doing business with governments.** Governments also create uncertainty in some markets when they run out of money toward the end of their budget year. A good case in point is California, which began to issue IOUs to its suppliers when its budget ran out and its legislature was unable to act. Consider how you would react if you received an IOU from a customer instead of payment.

- **Financial globalization.** Markets that have become globalized have additional risks in terms of changing exchange rates, timing, and settlement that are generated by differences in their legal system. Bankruptcy for the supplier as well as the buyer must be understood and monitored in terms of the laws of a particular country. A sourcing team must constantly monitor conditions within the geographical area of its suppliers (captured in an S2S system).

Implementing an S2S Process

"The devil is in the details," as the saying goes. When an organization decides to implement a system such as S2S, it has the option of purchasing and installing an existing software package from an outside source or creating its own. Sometimes it becomes apparent that we need to modify the existing software so that it more completely meets our operational needs. In doing so, we must pay particular attention to our business objectives so that we avoid overspecification (paying for features that are not required) and don't bog ourselves down in developing tactical minutiae. The benefit of an S2S system is its ability to drive process standardization and capture actionable information that is usually strategic in nature. This typically includes supplier performance, order status, spend analysis, cost control, outstanding contract obligations, and Accounts Payable status. We want this information so that we can meet strategic objectives, fulfill existing commitments to our end-user customers, reduce business and supplier risk, and work toward continuous process improvement.

Installing an S2S system is a means to an end objective(s) rather than the other way around. It is important to understand your organization's needs fully and analyze the market to determine exactly what sourcing is available to meet them. There is no substitute for thorough preparation; fully understanding our objectives and what we need to meet them. Such a process will reduce the cost of implementation, improve its chances of success, and provide the shortest path to a successful operational system. The point is simply this: Do your research homework.

This section provides a skeletal methodology for implementing an S2S process. Our goal is to help familiarize you with the overall requirements so that you know what to expect and can develop your own model for successful implementation.

Elements of a Source-to-Settle Process

Virtually all S2S software is modular. This means that the system can be implemented in multiple stages, depending on its architecture, of course. While all systems differ to one extent or another, a general pattern appears to emerge that establishes these key modules that need to be implemented.

SOURCING   Somewhat misleadingly named, most sourcing modules do not contain all the elements typically found in the process. Instead, they are most often designed to handle the simpler activities, such as supplier competitive bidding, requests for proposal, quotations, and perhaps electronic reverse auctions. However, suppliers must already be included in the system in order to participate. The systems we surveyed did not include important functions such as comparative supplier analysis, financial profiles (for risk management), capabilities, and current operational capacity levels. Some do include submodules for supplier rationalization (although most include this function in the analysis section).

PROCUREMENT   S2S software varies widely in this area, although most is characterized by electronic methodologies and applies only to indirect Maintenance, Repair, and Operations spending. The procurement module typically contains processes for these activities:

- Electronic catalogs containing prenegotiated items (Stock-Keeping Units) for use in selecting products (and, sometimes, services)
- Requisitioning by internal users and accompanying electronic work flow routing for approval that is based on preassigned levels of sign-off authority
- Assignment of purchases to department and general ledger codes
- Purchase order generation and electronic transmission to supplier using various methods, such as e-mail or "punch-out" (access to the supplier's portal along with the ability to select and order products) or through EDI
- Supplier order acknowledgment and Advanced Shipping Notices
- Shipping notice, delivery tracking and receiving

INVENTORY CONTROL   Typically used for manufacturing (direct spending), this module includes:

- Order releases to suppliers (on blanket purchase orders or Master Agreements)
- Receipt to stock and stock on hand (available and promised)
- Scheduled releases to manufacturing floor or stockrooms
- Valuation of inventory, on hand or in transit

- Inventory reconciliation with physical counts
- Returned authorizations to supplier

ACCOUNTING AND SETTLEMENT   This module includes all of the Accounts Payable functions:

- Invoice receipt and entry (or eInvoice)
- Debit memos and credit processing
- Electronic matching or invoice approval routing (for services)
- Discrepancy reconciliation
- Payment (by check or electronically)
- Tax accounting and payment
- Purchasing card management
- Financial cost accrual against purchase order commitments
- Budget interface

ANALYSIS   Using a variety of data mining management techniques, the analysis module provides standardized reports and information on demand. It typically includes:

- Spend analysis by product and supplier
- Usage data by cost center or department
- Supplier performance metrics
- Spending with noncontractual suppliers (maverick spending)
- Spending against budgets
- Spend variance of actual costs versus cost standards

Implementation Process

In order to smoothly implement an S2S system (or any complex process, for that matter), we need to utilize a cross-functional team consisting of stakeholders (users), subject matter experts, internal customers, and representatives from the Information Technology (IT) department. (In some cases, it might prove useful to have one or two supplier representatives, as well.) The project team must be in place prior to the system selection to ensure buy-in and business continuity. Here are the other recommended process steps.

REQUIREMENTS ANALYSIS   The using group typically establishes the requirements analysis via a Business Requirements Document (BRD) for the S2S system. Understanding the particular need based on factual data is critical to obtaining approval and funding. If you are part of the group leading the project, you will have already prepared a needs analysis to gain approval for the application from your management. If you are not part of this group, you will want to ensure that the project has been funded or appears likely to be funded so that you and your team can provide full support. If you are also a member of the sourcing team, you will want to see the BRD converted to a Statement of Work so that you can clearly determine the deliverables.

If a requirements analysis has not yet been performed, utilize the team to develop a detailed profile of existing conditions and the desired objectives. Gather the facts carefully so that there are no concerns regarding its accuracy:

- Create a process flow map; assess the cost and time it takes to perform the S2S process in its current state across the organization, using acceptably accurate data.
- Outline the key bottlenecks as pinch points.
- Determine how the project supports strategic business objectives.
- Estimate the resources needed (internal and external) to acquire and implement the S2S and support it going forward.
- Prepare an analysis of the Return on Investment and other benefits, such as improved customer support and supply management.

Two common traps should be avoided:

1. **Simply automating your current process because "it has worked in the past."** Implementing a S2S platform provides a unique opportunity to examine everything you do and to benchmark with best practices before going forward. Start from the ground and justify the value of every element that will go into the new process, whether it is an existing one or not. And listen to the provider of the proposed software: There may be new areas of metric tracking that you are not aware of and technology that can enable processes not considered previously.
2. **Failing to consult with your suppliers (existing or new) and to engage them in your analysis efforts.** Suppliers may have domain knowledge that you can leverage; some may have already implemented a similar system. You may even consider adding one or two to the S2S analysis team.

MANAGEMENT SUPPORT   Before going further, ensure that there is sufficient management support and that the project is funded. This should be done before investing time in performing the requirements analysis via a BRD from a logical viewpoint. It would be virtually impossible to gain management support without a justification analysis. Paradoxically, you may need some management buy-in before using any resources to go forward with the initial requirements analysis. However, if this is necessary, you may be able to present some compelling benchmarks (best practices) from other organizations that have already installed an S2S system or from published articles in various research organizations, trade magazines, and blogs.

MARKET RESEARCH It would be impossible to review all of the available solutions on the market. You can accelerate the selection process by using some basic approaches to finding the best solutions for your organization. Use the Internet to identify all available S2S systems. Since ongoing support is critical, carefully review and filter providers with programs less than a year or two old. Ask for a list of customers; find providers with customers in your industry or of your business size. Your short list should contain no more than five names; think of the aggregated amount of time you and the team will have to invest in reviewing each of them.

Avoid asking for a demonstration before you have finished your review and know which systems will best fit your organization's needs. It's easy to get sidetracked by some sales-oriented bells and whistles. Stick to your short list and provide each of the potential suppliers with your requirements documentation. Do this formally, using a Request for Proposal. Be sure to require respondents to use the format you have provided so that you can compare all of the proposals easily. Document everything, including conversations (formal and informal). Remember that verbal commitments must be included in the finalized written contract.

It will become apparent in reviewing proposals which providers can and cannot meet your requirements. Conduct a final shoot-out with no more than three that appear to have the systems closest to your needs. (Customization will be costly, so keep it to a minimum.) Ask for demonstrations within a specified time period. Check references with questions such as (but not limited to):

- How long did it take to implement your system?
- Did the supplier meet your timeline?
- Were costs in line with your expectations?
- Did you require more customization than expected?
- How well did your employees adapt to the new system?
- Have you achieved all of your sourcing objectives?
- Which sourcing objectives did you have to abandon?
- Does the supplier technology work as expected?
- Was the training effective and sufficient?
- Are you receiving the benefits you expected?
- Is the system operating to everyone's satisfaction?
- What do you believe could have been done better by the supplier?

- What do you believe could have been done better by your implementation team?

SELECTION   In making the final S2S supplier selection, thoroughly evaluate the proposals, the reference feedback, and the impressions of how close the systems come to matching stated requirements. Conduct a measured evaluation by each team member, summarize the findings, and select two suppliers (one primary and one fallback). There will not be full consensus; there rarely is. But you should be close enough to get buy-in from all user groups. If there are gaps between your needs and the system's capability, negotiate a solution that satisfies key internal customers. Make the award based on the viability of the system, the supplier's commitments to meeting the milestones in your timeline, and the supplier's proposed cost.

IMPLEMENTATION   If the selection process has been conducted properly, project implementation will be an extension of the processes outlined, and you can expect it to go smoothly—if you have a plan that everyone on the team agrees with. Here consensus is critical; you must mitigate any concerns by key users (including IT) regarding implementation methods, training, timelines, and communication. Some project management tips you might want to consider include:

- Develop the implementation plan, with an associated project timeline (with critical path items), in enough detail that it can be used as the guiding milestone document.
- Ensure that personnel resources will be available when needed.
- Establish a training plan and select superusers (subject matter experts) and end-user testers.
- Develop a communication plan. Determine who needs to know what and when.
- Implement the training and communications roll-out plans.
- Run a complete pilot on a test system.
- Populate the new system with required data.
- Run a pilot on the installed system.
- Have superusers try out the system with mock data.
- Run the new system in parallel with the existing system.
- Cut over to the new system, and retire the old one.
- Monitor operations with metrics to ensure service-level contract compliance.
- Review or survey the level of satisfaction by end users.
- Plan for additional tweaking and installation of planned module add-ons.

Please keep in mind that this list is not a guideline for implementation in itself. It is just meant to stimulate initial thought processes. And remember that rarely does an implementation go exactly as planned. Flexibility will stand everyone in good stead.

Managing the S2S Process

Aside from implementation, ongoing monitoring is one of the most important keys to achieving success with a process such as S2S. You must continually assess its effectiveness and iron out any wrinkles that appear.

A centralized management structure makes the process much easier to control; decentralization common to multiple operating units generally leads to a lack of adherence to the principles that drive anticipated benefits. We have come to recognize that decentralization results in redundant suppliers (and higher prices) and a decrease in contract compliance due to maverick spending.

Fully leveraging an S2S system requires some very tough management decisions. The organization can centralize operations under a single S2S officer and with a unified sourcing team. The sourcing team must become familiar with each unit's specific requirements so that it can develop relationships with suppliers that can effectively respond to the needs of each unit.

We often find that organizations are not willing to collectively buy in to a fully centralized sourcing, procurement, and contract administration group. This is quite understandable from an internal user's perspective. So what is the solution? Many organizations find that a central sourcing group, with team members located in each of the major business units, can effectively unify the supplier selection and management and the initial selection and contracting process. Individual business units usually maintain a dedicated procurement team to handle local requirements. The enabling factor is linking all groups together through the same system and process. This way, all sourcing and procurement personnel have access to the same data at the same time.

Supplier selection and supplier management is often conducted by dispersed sourcing and commodity management teams. For geographically dispersed units, suppliers must have the capability of serving all of them, or at least those that account for 90 percent utilization and above. This requirement for suppliers to serve all of an organization's locations tends to provide some management challenges for them, but the challenges so far have proven manageable through increased communication via today's online collaboration tools and additional travel for face-to-face meetings by the staff.

Outsourcing the S2S Process

Organizations today are increasingly turning to Business Process Outsourcing for many of the services they use that do not fall within the scope of their core competencies. Sourcing and procurement of indirect goods and services, along with the management of the S2S system, are becoming more and more prevalent, and with increasingly effective results.

There must be a clear benefit to outsourcing these functions in order to gain management's interest. BPO providers must be selected on their demonstrated ability to ensure operational effectiveness. But as experience increases, organizations are better equipped to make the right decisions, select outsourced groups with excellent track records, and acquire the ability to become effective managers of the outsourced business processes.

Despite the somewhat increased risk, organizations still find many benefits in outsourcing the acquisition of indirect goods and services. Reduced operational cost is quite possibly the most important benefit organizations seek. Most outsourcing services are simply better at what they do than most of their customers. Outsourcing companies are also better equipped to effectively absorb spikes in transactional volume since they generally employ a larger staff than their customers. From a finance perspective, this outsourcing means that a variable cost can be transferred to a fixed cost, and we always know the cost of outsourced operations.

In the sourcing and procurement functions, outsourcing can also provide a smoother overall operation. Outsourcing providers are able to hire more focused and highly specialized employees since they work with larger overall volumes. Working with many customers and many suppliers gives them access to benchmarking information previously available only to major consulting firms (many of which are today engaged in providing outsourced services themselves). As a result of their increased volumes, outsourcing firms are also better able to acquire the best technology, generally unaffordable by most small and midsize organizations.

Summary

We began this chapter with a detailed analysis of the reasons why organizations need an S2S system. The issues presented included the lack of uniform processes and the lack of compliance to business process policy.

The objectives and benefits of an S2S process include cost reduction/ cost avoidance, increased spend visibility, better regulatory compliance, standardized processes, reduced transaction costs, improved supplier integration, and risk management.

Then we covered the basics of implementing an S2S process, describing the elements of an S2S process, including sourcing, procurement, inventory control, accounting and settlement, and analysis. The implementation process includes a requirements analysis, management support, market research, system selection, and bringing the system online.

We concluded with some notes on managing the S2S process and important considerations in outsourcing.

CHAPTER 4

Cultural Considerations
for Global Sourcing

The sourcing processes examined in this book are affected significantly by the different cultures that employ them. A sourcing method that works in one country may not work in another, simply because business is conducted differently in those countries. However, cultural variation in the conduct of business from one country to another is, in itself, an enormous body of knowledge, the subject of many books and papers so we approach it in this chapter with a broad brush. Considering that there are 195 countries in the world (as of this writing), it would be virtually impossible to cover each country in detail. What is important, we believe, is that our review may help to increase your awareness of the role that culture plays in the conduct of normal international business relations.

Let's begin with an explanation: By "cultural," we mean those forms of etiquette and, perhaps, beliefs that are associated with a cohesive social or organizational group. It is their *shared* beliefs and the manner in which they *behave* toward one another that really interests us. Keep in mind, though, that to some extent, business conduct is also influenced by many other factors, such as regional traditions, ethnicity, nationality, religion, social group, government, educational background, and industry. This is where you must look to gain an understanding of what is important and what is not in any given culture ideology.

In Chapter 12 we provide the specific business details of sourcing globally, such as regulations, payment methods, Customs and duties, risk, and other important elements of international trade.

Conducting Business in Other Nations

If you intend to conduct business in a country that is not your own or with which you are unfamiliar, it would be well worthwhile to study its culture as thoroughly as possible. Look for instructional material that focuses on how business is conducted in the particular country where you are sourcing. For example, in some countries, relationships must be formed first, prior to any business discussions or transactions. Doing this may mean socializing to some extent so that you and your business counterpart have a chance to get to know one another. In some countries, business is business, and socializing is unacceptable. We often refer to these preferences as "cultural values." In the next section, we examine these values in more detail.

Cultural Values

In developing an approach to global sourcing in an unfamiliar country, you should spend some time gathering important facts about its culture. Focus on actual examples rather than statements of the country's ideal set of values; often there is a large gap between actuality and ideals. You want to be prepared for what you will actually encounter in the real world of business. Try to sort out what is important for you to know about conducting business in that culture. If socializing will be part of your visit, be sure you understand some of the key protocols and make up a checklist of do's and don'ts. Please see the Suggested Reading section at the end of this book for a short list of resources that may assist your research into the culture of a particular country. To help you get started, though, the following sections provide an outline of some important factors to look into.

Organizational and Social Culture

It is not surprising to discover that many organizations have a relatively distinct culture. For example, it is easy to distinguish the Apple culture from the culture at HP. Apple's culture is characterized by fervent employee dedication and is well known for its innovation and the secrecy with which it develops new products. Apple is also led by its longtime chief executive officer (CEO), Steve Jobs, who, in many circles, is virtually a cult figure. At HP, employee dedication is not displayed quite so fanatically, and its strong culture of developing new products does not focus on game-changing technology. Its founders and, perhaps, one or two of its past CEOs are relatively well known, but many of the others are far from being household names.

Within the same organization, however, the culture is often modified by the country in which the particular facility is located. Work habits vary from country to country; facilities in Japan and China, for example, provide private offices for only the most senior executives while in the United States virtually every manager has one. Time off varies widely too: In the United States, employees are content with two or three weeks vacation each year, while in Europe the general standard is six weeks. Keep in mind, too, the importance of holidays in each of the countries in which you are sourcing. Doing so will help direct your awareness to traditions that are culturally important in that country.

How does organizational culture come about? Edgar Schein, in his book *Organizational Culture and Leadership: A Dynamic View*, points out that an organization's culture develops to help it cope with its environment. This means that corporate culture derives its fundamental characteristics from the social culture in which it operates. There are many, many examples of social culture becoming manifest within organizations. In fact, the effective organization will actually employ measures that help adapt its operations to conditions within the social structure of the country or its geographical location.

Unless you reside within a particular society, it will be very difficult to understand all of its nuances and drivers. But it should not be very difficult to learn how the company we are engaged with adapts that culture to its business processes and ways of conducting business.

ORGANIZATIONAL STRUCTURE   How employees interact with one another can be an indication of the organizational structure and reflect its cultural norms. In some organizations, there is a very well-defined organizational structure; in others, roles are very loosely defined. In an organization with a highly functioning hierarchy where decisions are made from the top down, roles are much more formal, and it generally takes longer to make decisions.

Is the organization structured around specific business functions, such as manufacturing or design? Can you determine which functions or departments are the most important to the organization's executive management? If so, how are customers served? In an organization that has a well-defined customer service function, there is a specific avenue, a bureaucratic protocol system, for assistance. Without a dedicated customer-oriented function, service may be a matter of tapping into your relationship with an executive or sales account manager.

INDIVIDUAL ROLES   Is the individual's status important to the organization? If so, this should be demonstrated by working conditions and the extent to which the organization encourages a work/life balance. When an organization values its employees as individuals and encourages individual thinking, there is typically a higher degree of innovation and a greater willingness to take on higher levels of responsibility. Without emphasis on the individual, organizations tend to be more bureaucratic and generally slower to respond to customers' requests. However, the slower disciplined path often means greater reliability. Which of the two approaches is best for your own organization is a decision that you will have to make.

CONFLICT RESOLUTION   Conflict, like culture itself, is often hard to discern. By "conflict" we mean disagreements and disputes between business partners, rather than conflicts arising from competition. Virtually all cultures deal with conflict differently. In some cultures, conflict is never allowed to surface; in others, there is great sensitivity to airing out conflicts and having them resolved. In the United States, as an example, dispute resolution is an integral part of most business-to-business contracts. There are established procedures such as mediation, arbitration, and, ultimately, the courts.

The importance of resolving business disputes cannot be overemphasized. History is filled with examples of countries going to war over commercial interests. To some extent, the early European settlement of U.S. territories outside the original 13 colonies can be characterized by wars between nations that developed from private business interests.

As part of any sourcing project, it is important to understand both the cultural and the legal nature of conflict and conflict resolution in business that is conducted in another country. You can most often do this research through Internet browsing or resources in the commerce branches of potential partners' governments.

DRESS REQUIREMENTS   Today, many businesses around the world have adopted a more relaxed approach to dress codes. But this is not always the case; some societies continue to expect more formal attire. In Saudi Arabia, for example, despite the heat, men are expected to wear suits and ties when attending business meetings. Women are expected to wear business suits (with a dress rather than pants); skirts should reach well below the knee and, better still, to the ankle. Throughout the Middle East and in countries with Muslim populations, women should have a head scarf or shawl readily available.

You will never go wrong by overdressing, but you can leave a very poor impression by dressing down when it is not considered culturally appropriate.

TREATMENT OF VISITORS   In some countries, business visitors are treated as guests with a great deal of reverence and respect. Hosting a dinner or lunch for you is viewed as a relished social pleasure, and getting to know you is an important consideration. You may be treated like a celebrity and asked many questions in the attempt to get to know you on a personal basis. Often meals include domestic alcohol, and you will be expected to imbibe. The alcoholic strength of locally produced beverages varies widely so be cautious: How you handle its effect may reflect poorly on you at a later time.

The celebrity distinction often breaks down after a time, as the parties conduct business and get to know one another. This is not a bad sign and should be expected. Be aware, however, that often the host continues to pick up the bill for meals and entertainment. It would be impolite to suggest paying or even splitting the bill. When you are the host, you will be expected to cover the events tab.

In some cultures, gift giving is an accepted process, especially when receiving visitors or when making visits to others. Generally, the value of the gift is not important, but in some countries, you need to be sure to give the gifts that may be seen to have more value to the senior managers rather than buying the same types of items for everyone.

It is also very important to become familiar with the accepted form of arrival greeting. In Japan, it is common practice to bow briefly from the waist when meeting, with the lower-ranking individual making the lowest bow. In Germany, a very firm handshake is required, both when greeting and when leaving.

The exchange of business cards is a formal affair in many cultures. When you accept the person's card, read it for a few moments before putting it away. Simply putting the card in your pocket or briefcase can be taken as a sign of disrespect, leaving the impression that you have no interest in the person's being or rank.

DELEGATION OF AUTHORITY   The nature and degree of authority varies quite widely from culture to culture. In the United States, for example, it is common practice for companies to delegate authority to individuals to select suppliers and to execute contracts for acquisitions up to a specific dollar amount. In some countries, however, it is always the most senior manager who approves any contractual agreement. In other countries—Japan, for example—decisions are most often made by a group consensus that includes all members of the affected sourcing team.

The "Definition" of Authority

During a time when technology was being reinvented virtually every day, we found ourselves without a supplier for a key component. We were late in making our needs known for a new product, and our primary supplier had committed all of its capacity to others.

(continued)

(continued)

Our sourcing manager knew of a company in Japan that could fill our requirement and likely had open capacity. It was not the most cost-effective solution, we were told, but we were in a bind. Fortunately, the company had a local representative, actually a vice president (VP), in the United States so we immediately invited him to discuss our needs. As usual, time was of the essence, so we strategized how we might accelerate the typical Japanese style of making decisions by consensus.

The supplier's VP came to our facility the very next day, and we conducted the appropriate ceremonies. Our strategy was direct: We asked if the VP had the authority to conduct such negotiations unilaterally. He said he did. We then asked if he had the authority to sign the contract. He said he did again. We were ecstatic.

We soon came to an agreement on terms and pricing. We had our contract manager bring in a standard supply contract, we signed it and passed it over to the supplier's VP for signature. What he said then took us totally off guard. He told us that he had to fax the contract to Japan for review and that it would take several days before it could be signed.

But, we said, didn't you tell us you had the authority to negotiate the contract and the authority to sign it? Yes, he said he did, we were correct in both cases. He told us the contract that he had just negotiated had to go to the home office for team review before he would sign it.

We were left wondering what we had missed.

Ethics/Code of Business Conduct/Social Responsibility

Ethics and its related imperatives of business conduct and social responsibility are concepts that vary widely around the world. Some of the concepts are driven by religious beliefs; others are related to tradition and law. Unfortunately, there is currently no universal standard that can guide us.

In this section, we are going to examine the fundamental principles behind these concepts without discussing how they are, or should be, applied. It is a matter for you and your organization's management to determine if local codes and traditions are in line with your policy and personal views and in line with governmental requirements.

BUSINESS ETHICS Originally conceived in philosophy, the term "ethics" has come to mean a body of moral principles we adopt within our culture as a common standard of guidance. Like culture itself, ethics binds various elements of a society together through commonly held moral beliefs of right and wrong, good and bad, what constitutes justice or virtue.

When we speak about ethics in a business context, we are referring to the principles, or morals, used to guide individuals and organizations in the conduct of their commercial activities. More specifically, ethics applies primarily to the decision-making process. Ethical imperatives (or their absence) are critical elements in an organization's approach to doing business. Because business ethics are not always contained in a formal code, you will need to research how they apply to the country and organization you are considering. There is no universally accepted code of ethics.

In assessing an organization's approach to ethical behavior, you will want to try to answer a number of questions. You may want to use this list as a starting point:

- What influences decisions?
- How important is compliance with the law?
- What is the importance of the family in business decisions?
- Are employees treated with respect? At all levels?
- What is the importance of employee health and safety?
- How are supplier relationships viewed?
- Do employees respect their managers?
- Are employees loyal to their employer?
- Is professional competence as important as connections?
- Do minorities receive respect and equal treatment?
- Does the organization have a set of principles requiring compliance?
- How are conflicts of interest regarded?
- Is confidentiality valued?

CODE OF BUSINESS CONDUCT Within an organization, ethical guidance is often required to ensure a uniform system of behavior. Generally this is manifested in a Code of Conduct, a written set of rules telling all employees what is required behavior in various circumstances.

It is not uncommon for U.S. and European as well as multinational organizations to have a written code to guide their employees and to ensure compliance to a uniform set of standards. However, the concept is far from universal. Many countries rely on strong religious beliefs to guide their behavior instead of turning to their employers. In other countries, the concept is not considered. In sourcing, you need to determine what applies to your business dealings as well as the strength and importance of a uniform guide to business conduct.

SOCIAL RESPONSIBILITY In its broader sense, the term "social responsibility" refers to a set of organizational policies and procedures intended to improve the environment, the community, the organization, and the workplace. When such policies and procedures become formalized, we refer to them as a Code of Social Responsibility, a doctrine that is closely related to ethical behavior and business conduct in its method of providing guidance.

However, whether formalized or not, an organization's approach to social responsibility should be evaluated as an important element of sourcing. There are a number of elements to be considered.

Environmental Responsibility   With the focus on global warming and carbon emissions, environmental concerns have come to the forefront of our sourcing evaluations. Businesses are increasingly focusing on "green" processes in their operations, processes that reduce the harm to the environment, and insist that their suppliers do the same. Unfortunately, there is much controversy surrounding the reduction of unsustainable practices, such as pollution and chemical emissions, and countries have not been able to formulate a universal policy.

"Sustainability" is a term used to describe the manner in which we return resources to our ecological systems so that they are available to us on a continuing basis—a seemingly simple concept. Adherence to sustainable practices in the use of resources has become an important element in the protection of the environment. Many organizations, lacking governmental support, have taken it on themselves to provide leadership to this cause.

However, there have been a number of attempts to voluntarily codify environmental responsibility by organizations with a global outlook:

- The ISO (International Organization for Standardization) 14000 series is described by the U.S. Environmental Protection Agency (EPA) as a standard requiring "that a community or organization put in place and implement a series of practices and procedures that, when taken together, result in an Environmental Management System (EMS)." The major requirements of an EMS under ISO 14001, the EPA goes on to say, contains:

  - *A policy statement which includes commitments to prevention of pollution, continual improvement of the EMS leading to improvements in overall environmental performance, and compliance with all applicable statutory and regulatory requirements.*
  - *Identification of all aspects of the community organization's activities, products, and services that could have a significant impact on the environment, including those that are not regulated.*
  - *Setting performance objectives and targets for the management system which link back to the three commitments established in the*

community or organization's policy (i.e., prevention of pollution, continual improvement, and compliance).
- *Implementing the EMS to meet these objectives. This includes activities like training of employees, establishing work instructions and practices, and establishing the actual metrics by which the objectives and targets will be measured.*
- *Establishing a program to periodically audit the operation of the EMS.*
- *Checking and taking corrective and preventive actions when deviations from the EMS occur, including periodically evaluating the organization's compliance with applicable regulatory requirements.*
- *Undertaking periodic reviews of the EMS by top management to ensure its continuing performance and making adjustments to it, as necessary.*

—Voluntary Environmental Management Systems/ISO 14001, *Frequently Asked Questions*, United States Environmental Protection Agency,www.epa.gov/owm/iso14001/isofaq.htm.

- The United Nations Global Compact, also known as Compact or UNGC, is a United Nations program that encourages businesses to adopt a universal set of principles. It is characterized by ten principles:

The Ten Principles

Human Rights

Principle 1: Businesses should support and respect the protection of internationally proclaimed human rights.
Principle 2: Make sure that they are not complicit in human rights abuses.

Labor Standards

Principle 3: Businesses should uphold the freedom of association and the effective recognition of the right to collective bargaining.
Principle 4: The elimination of all forms of forced and compulsory labor.
Principle 5: The effective abolition of child labor.
Principle 6: The elimination of discrimination in respect of employment and occupation.

Environment

Principle 7: Businesses should support a precautionary approach to environmental challenges.
Principle 8: Undertake initiatives to promote greater environmental responsibility.
Principle 9: Encourage the development and diffusion of environmentally friendly technologies.

Anti-Corruption

Principle 10: Businesses should work against corruption in all its forms, including extortion and bribery.

Source: "The Ten Principles." United Nations. www.unglobalcompact.org/aboutthegc/thetenprinciples/index.html.

Legal Aspects of Sourcing We have seen numerous contracts with overseas trading partners initiated by U.S. businesses that emanate from the Uniform Commercial Code (UCC). Most of the time these contracts have no official legal standing in countries other than the United States. Fortunately, most businesses, regardless of their locations, value the goodwill of their customers and so we find only isolated cases of litigation. It is important, however, to consult an attorney familiar with the legal system in the country you are sourcing in, before beginning the contracting process.

A useful guide is the United Nations Convention on Contracts for the International Sale of Goods (CISG). CISG is the equivalent of the UCC in the United States (but by no means a parallel) and can be used for the same purposes (i.e., contract formation). Though only 74 countries have agreed to its provisions, those countries account for a significant proportion of world trade.

Sourcing Challenges

For the sourcing professional, few activities are more daunting than evaluating business culture in another country. There is so much to learn. What follows is far from a definitive review of the challenges you will face by doing business in another country. We hope it will provide a starting point to stimulate thought and begin additional research.

Communication

Although English is generally accepted as the global business language, there will be situations where the individual you are dealing with struggles to translate his or her own thoughts. You can handle this two ways: (1) Exercise profound patience and perhaps help the individual put words to thoughts when appropriate, or (2) use a translator, typically someone from outside the individual's organization who will not be overly biased or sensitive to the contact's rank.

It never hurts to learn a few phrases in the predominant language of the country you are visiting. Except in rare circumstances, your poor pronunciation will not be held against you and people will appreciate your attempts. Be careful, though: Sometimes a mispronounced word can lend an entirely different meaning than what you intended. Try your skill with a neutral party before trying it with your contact.

BODY LANGUAGE Body language, perhaps one of the more fascinating aspects of cultural variation, can be a highly useful tool in dealing with cultures other than your own. It is an essential element of communication, and there certainly are many facets to consider in doing business in other countries . . . and seemingly unlimited variations.

In China, you may notice what appears to be a general attitude of indifference. However, as most observers with strong backgrounds in Chinese business habits will tell you, they are far from passive. Westerners unfortunately fail to understand the culture: The Chinese tend to display very little body language in their reactions; we need to learn to understand them.

The use of the eyes can have opposite effects from one country to another. For example, in the United States, direct eye contact, especially when meeting for the first time, is considered a sign of openness and a desire to establish trust. In Japan, however, it is considered rude; the Japanese tend to focus their gaze on the neck.

There are endless examples of how body language varies in different cultures. Before traveling to another country, it would be best to study and practice the use of body language in that particular environment. As always, there is no substitute for preparation.

USE OF COMMUNICATION TECHNOLOGY There is little doubt that technology has had a dramatic effect on communication. In fact, we recognize that the globalization of communication is a direct result of the technology that enables it. But has the expansion of communication technology had a similar impact on the culture of a particular society?

TABLE 4.1 East/West Difference in Emoticons

Emotion	West	East
"Happy"	:-)	(ˆ _ ˆ)
"Sad"	:-(	(;_;) or (T_T)
"Surprise"	:-o	(o.o)

Technology has become the great unifier, providing immediate access to new information by anyone with access to the internet or a cell phone. Consider the increase in the speed of communication in just the past 25 years. One can only wonder how this technology has homogenized culture among developed nations and segments of nations that are still developing around the globe. Although societies have been communicating with one another across millennia and have so far managed to maintain their individuality, it is important to understand that the evolution of technology has had a revolutionary effect on society, both culturally and politically. Where technology is accessible, it is definitely changing how businesses operate and how they are able to interact.

Global Communication: An Anecdote

I received a call on my cell phone at about 6:30 PM (Pacific) as I was pulling into my driveway after work. It was the account representative from a company that was having production problems and was late on an important shipment to my company. He was calling to say that the problem had been resolved and that the shipment would be on its way in a couple of hours. This prompted me to ask what time zone he was in. I was surprised to learn it was early morning in Guangzhou, China, and, calling me on his cell phone, he had just left home for his office.

Does this incident demonstrate that the content and comprehension of our communication has become globally unified? Table 4.1 shows some information taken from a BBC online discussion in August 2008 that may provide evidence that societies will continue to develop their individuality.

Concept of Time

The concept of time is another element that must be considered during sourcing activities. Time is most definitely a cultural variation. The concept of time varies widely from culture to culture and may, in fact, separate people and affect how they conduct themselves. In the West we are time driven. Time is linear and measured in standard increments. It permeates our lives and becomes intrinsically bound in our most fundamental objectives.

In the East, however, time feels unlimited, continuously uncoiling rather than constricted by linear boundaries. In India, for example, it is said that time flows endlessly and there is an awareness that it stretches far beyond our comprehension. Imagine a bird picking up a grain of sand from a beach and flying it to the other side of the earth; eternity just begins when that bird has picked up every grain of sand on every beach on our planet and flown it around to the other side of the world.

This idea goes deeply to the heart of one of the most common Western business concepts, that "time is of the essence" in fulfilling a contractual obligation. Ask yourself: How will this be interpreted by your counterpart in another country?

Conducting Negotiations

Negotiation processes and styles vary widely from place to place. The question you must ask is: How are negotiations conducted in this country? For example, the process may be formal or informal. In a formal process, chances are you will be reviewing the proposal or contract line by line. You may find that your potential supplier has several colleagues taking part, each with a particular role (e.g., engineering, finance, and manufacturing). You may be invited by your host to share a meal before beginning any discussions about the work. In some countries, especially in some Middle Eastern countries, a handshake at the end of what you think is the negotiation is really just the end of the informal process—the agreement to agree—and the beginning of actual contractual negotiations on pricing and terms.

In many cultures around the world, individuals may find it hard to say no. It is considered impolite, if not rude, so when working in such an environment, phrase your questions in a way that does not require a yes or no answer.

Intellectual Property

The ownership of intellectual property has become one of the most difficult issues in global commerce that has yet to be fully resolved. Intellectual property, so highly valued and controlled in the West, is a very different concept in other cultures, one that can be hard to characterize. It is important to understand that laws and attitudes vary widely. In the Suggested Reading section at the end of this book, you will find some references that may help you sort out the dangers of trying to control intellectual property in dissimilar cultures. The outcome of your sourcing effort may depend on your knowledge of how intellectual property ownership is regarded in the country in which you are planning to conduct business.

Summary

Understanding cultural influences in business relationships is critical to any sourcing effort, and especially so when working with organizations in another country. In this chapter, we explored some of the more important aspects of cultural influences in conducting business abroad. We examined concepts of conducting business in other nations, such as cultural values. In doing so, we considered aspects of organizational and social culture along with organizational structure, the role of the individual, conflict resolution, dress requirements, treatment of visitors, and delegation of authority. We also looked at ethics in business, codes of business conduct, and social responsibility, including environmental responsibility, as well as some of the legal aspects to be considered in sourcing. Turning then to a discussion of sourcing challenges, we pointed out the important roles of communication and its associated technology, concluding with an overview of time concepts, conducting negotiations, and intellectual property. Much of this information will be expanded upon in other chapters.

CHAPTER 5

Supplier Research
and Market Analysis

I n this chapter, we examine two related concepts that are essential to any sourcing project: supplier research and market analysis. As used in our approach, which divides the two segments, supplier research is the process of obtaining information for sources specific to the *item* (product or service) being acquired in order to facilitate competitive practices and supplier selection. Market analysis is the process of gathering relevant information from economic indicators and emerging trends within the particular *industry* and the competitive environment of the product or service we are sourcing. In doing so, we can generate a picture or model of the marketplace so that individual supplier qualifications and performance can be assessed in terms of not only the organization's requirements, but what is commercially available for purchase as well. Supplier research and market analysis, taken together, provide the basis for us to understand what products and services are available, who the most qualified potential suppliers are, and how the market for that particular product or service operates.

Conducting Supplier Research

Supplier research is used in sourcing for two main purposes:

1. **To identify *qualifiable* suppliers or contractors that can provide goods or services to our organization.** By "qualifiable," we mean suppliers that have been screened and meet the capability, financial, and capacity requirements for the current requirement. These suppliers have not yet been certified or formally approved by the sourcing selection team.

2. **To determine an appropriate strategy for solicitation, evaluation, and assembling the bidders' list.** This strategy is based on both supplier research and market research, which, taken together, establishes the basis for our acquisition and sourcing plan.

Methods and Techniques for Locating Potential Suppliers

How difficult is it to find supplier sourcing information? Well, not really difficult at all if you know where to look. Let's see where we can find sources.

In developing a further understanding of the market, we can leverage a number of sources (apart from the companies themselves) to provide additional insight and information. We can include:

- **Experts.** These should include in-house expertise and commodity centers.
- **Current suppliers.** Often they have in-house category information and solutions that may meet your sourcing requirements.
- **Other recent market research.** Check files for similar purchases.
- **Requests for information.** These are formal methods for obtaining comparative data.
- **The Internet.** Although the Internet is a useful source of information, you must be careful to avoid broad search engines that can provide information overload. Instead, use sites that aggregate catalogs from many similar suppliers. You can use these catalogs for convenient side-by-side comparisons.
- **Online databases.** Industry web sites and consolidated catalog sites provide useful information.
- **Source lists from other sections within your organization.**
- **Product literature.** Often you must specifically request such data from the supplier, but sometimes you can find it easily on the supplier's web site.
- **Trade shows.** Although attendance is time consuming and often requires travel, trade shows can be especially valuable when sourcing new products that will be used extensively and potential new sources of supply.
- **Professional associations.** For example, the National Institute for Automotive Service Excellence and the Institute of Electrical and Electronic Engineers (IEEE) maintain product standards.
- **Market research firms.** Many companies specialize in developing detailed market analysis along with specific commodity research and sell the results.

Have in front of you a detailed description of what it is you are sourcing and what requirement you need it for. The description should include its function, performance requirements, and any other characteristics that are critical. In addition, keep in mind any alternatives or modifications that can be made using commercially available products or services where a trade-off is possible. Always keep in mind the delivery schedule: When do you need the product or service, and how critical are those dates to satisfy the requirement?

For your own documentation and perhaps for some audit review that may occur in the future, keep track of whom you contacted for advice (e.g., industry experts), the names of the firms or organizations you contacted for evaluation, and those suppliers on your final, short finalist list.

DIRECTORIES AND INDUSTRIAL GUIDES The most traditional means of locating potential suppliers is through industry-focused directories and buyers' guides. These are typically published in conjunction with a trade magazine or an industry association and contain listings of suppliers grouped by specialty or geographical location. They also often contain information about suppliers' products or services, capabilities, size, and market segment, along with contact names, e-mail addresses, web site URLs, and telephone numbers.

One of the most commonly used directories is the *Thomas Register*, a general directory covering several hundred industries and hundreds of thousands of suppliers. Other directories are focused more specifically on one particular industry, such as those published by *Ceramic Industry* magazine directed at the ceramic manufacturing industry and the Buyers' Guide published by *Electronics Weekly* magazine.

The ever-popular telephone directories, such as the local Yellow Pages, provide listings of businesses for a local calling area by category but typically provide no specific information beyond the advertising paid for by the organization. Regional business directories published by local newspapers to promote business in the readership area are also popular.

INTERNET SEARCH TOOLS Today, it is common to use the Internet to search for suppliers. Using easily accessed search engines such as Google, you can locate multiple suppliers for any product or service simply by entering product key words in the search. The problem, as you may have already experienced, is that there is so much information available on the Internet that it can be impractical to search through it all. For example, a Google search for the phrase "paper cup manufacturer" returned 130,000 entries in less than one second.

TRADE ASSOCIATIONS/TRADE SHOWS   Trade organizations typically sponsor magazines and online directories that help the buyer find sources. More important, perhaps, these organizations sponsor local or national trade shows that bring together all of the significant suppliers within a specific industry for several days of workshops and exhibits where buyers can contact a significant number of suppliers in one location. An example is Electronics West, an annual exhibit held on the West Coast for electronic component suppliers. This trade show brings together hundreds of established and newly organized companies that supply the electronics OEM (original equipment manufacturer) marketplace and is cosponsored by several professional organizations, including the IEEE.

GOVERNMENTAL AGENCIES   Many governmental agencies provide information and directories that can be used for sourcing. The most commonly available are those published by the U.S. Department of Commerce and the U.S. General Services Administration's Federal Supply Service.

MINORITY SUPPLIER DIRECTORIES   For those seeking minority suppliers, literally dozens of minority business directories are available, many through local minority business councils. One of the most useful directories is released by the U.S. Small Business Administration online at www.sba8a.com.
There are two other places to look for minority suppliers:

1. The National Minority Supplier Development Council was chartered in 1972 to provide increased procurement and business opportunities for minority businesses of all sizes (www.nmsdc.org).
2. The National Minority Business Council was founded in 1972 as a full-service, nonprofit corporation. The organization is dedicated to providing business assistance, educational opportunities, seminars, purchasing listings and related services to hundreds of businesses across the United States (www.nmbc.org).

CONSULTANTS   When a significant or critical need arises and there are no internal resources to provide adequate sourcing domain expertise, procurement professionals often reach outside the organization for proven expertise. Engaging consultants who are industry experts can save time on finding and preparing detailed studies and comparisons of sources, since they already have substantial knowledge of suppliers and can leverage their expertise to decrease the time it takes to develop the best supplier fit. Although hiring consultants might appear to be an expensive approach, in the long run it can save valuable time and expense.

Gathering Information

Enormous amounts of data are available, and often analyzing those data becomes confusing and difficult. For this reason, the information that is obtained needs to be cataloged and organized to prevent information overload.

We can organize the important information we obtain by our supplier research into several major categories, as described in the following sections.

FINANCIAL AND BUSINESS DATA   Our primary concern is the supplier's ability to support our business, so we want to assemble factual material that we can use to make an assessment. Doing this is relatively straightforward when looking at a publicly held corporation, since the Securities and Exchange Commission requires the regular publication of virtually all of the necessary data. For a privately held company, however, the data may not be so easy to obtain; nevertheless it is important for critical suppliers. Often such information is available through Dun & Bradstreet, a traditional provider of financial and risk-management information addressing corporate solvency, or a similar service.

We are primarily examining historical documents to determine the company's financial health, its rate of growth (a possible danger signal if it is unsustainable), and its business interests. Some questions that we should be able to answer include:

- What is its position in the market (market share, volume, and cost position)?
- Who are its customers?
- How profitable is it, and what are its profit trends?
- What is its financial health (as shown on the balance sheet)? Trends?
- Does it pay its obligations on time?
- Who owns the company?
- Are there any legal liens or other legal proceedings currently active?
- What are its policies for social responsibility? Does it actively support sustainability?
- Is it diversified? To what degree is it vertically integrated?
- What are its short-term and long-term business goals and strategies (and do they align with ours)?
- Are the key materials (and labor) it uses volatile or single/sole sourced?
- How much above break-even is it operating?
- What is its pricing structure? Does it vary by product or market?
- What is its financial risk profile?
- In what country is it located?

In addition to answering these questions (and others you may have), compare some of its key financial ratios, such as the Quick Ratio/Current Ratio, Return on Net Assets, Gross/Net Margins and Overhead to Sales, to those of other suppliers of similar size in the industry.

TECHNOLOGY   Typically, the sourcing group will rely on internal expertise to determine the nature of the technology the potential supplier employs (internally) and, if it operates in a technologically focused industry, whether it is an innovation leader or follower. Are we going to pay a premium for leading-edge technology? What is the estimated life cycle of the technology?

We will also want to consider the nature of its intellectual property, including patent holdings, operating systems, and trade secrets. How does the intellectual property provide a competitive advantage? Are the company's patents properly protected for the future?

MANUFACTURING AND DISTRIBUTION   As with technology, in assessing the potential supplier's manufacturing and distribution capabilities, we will also want to employ some specialized knowledge through our internal staff or through a focused market research project. All of the information we get needs to be compared with the supplier's key competitors to develop a clear picture of its position. Some of the questions we can ask include:

- What is the age and geographical location of its facilities?
- What is the age of its equipment, and how long is its expected life span?
- What share of its production volume and capacity does the product line we use require?
- Overall, what is its production capacity, and to what extent is it being used?
- Is the product (or service) we intend to purchase a central core competency for this supplier?
- Are its production processes proprietary or based on some common process standard?
- What are its lead times compared with others in the industry?
- How are its products distributed? Do they employ direct sales or sales through a wholesaler/distributor?
- Are its distribution points strategically located on a domestic or global basis?

GOVERNANCE/ORGANIZATION   Another important attribute to consider is how decisions are made within the potential supplier's organization. Are decisions made centrally, or are they delegated to operating personnel in business units? How long is the chain of command? The answers to these questions may provide insight into the length of time it will take to ratify key decisions affecting your procurement and supplier selections. And along these lines, we should determine our points of contact and their position within the company. How will our voice, as a customer, be heard and taken into account?

In this category, we might also include the potential supplier's obligations under law. Is it clearly in compliance with its country's governmental regulations? What is its litigation record? Are there any significant legal or regulatory violations, and are they still outstanding? This is another way of assessing some important supplier risk factors.

BUSINESS RELATIONSHIPS Any consideration of supplier capabilities must take into account the company's important strategic business relationships, including its customers and suppliers as well as its consultants and analysts. Is it part of any joint ventures or consortiums? If so, how might this affect our business relationship?

Importantly, what is its relationship to its employees and contractors? Is the morale high or low? Is it unionized? If so, what is its working history? Are there any workforce grievances? Is it on good terms with the unions?

We might also want to understand the company's relationships with its local government and how well it is supported as an important member of the community. Does it meet its obligations for social responsibility? Are its employees respected in the community?

LOCAL, DOMESTIC, OR INTERNATIONAL Sourcing decisions based on a supplier's location often provide distinct advantages in specific situations. A local supplier, for example, may feel a greater obligation to maintain higher levels of service because it shares the same community as the buyer. And buying organizations may have the same preference for supporting other members of the immediate community. Local suppliers, too, can frequently provide faster response time as well as lower freight costs.

The buying organization can develop greater competition simply by expanding the geographical range of its sourcing to national and international sources that may provide better pricing and wider choices.

Similarly, there are numerous trade-offs to consider when making a decision to source domestically or internationally. Typically, communications and delivery are more reliable with domestic sources, whereas international sources can usually provide lower prices due to reduced labor costs.

There are also payment methods to consider when evaluating offshore or domestic sources. Commonly, sellers will want overseas buyers to guarantee payment through some form of bank document, such as a Letter of Credit (LC). An LC usually contains provisions triggering an automatic payment from the buyer's bank upon documented proof of shipment or at some specific predetermined time interval. This can be a relatively costly process and can tie up cash or credit lines for an inordinate period of time.

In addition, we must consider any additional risks that may arise due to fluctuations in currency exchange rates when purchasing internationally. Long-term contracts often contain a clause that adjusts the selling price based on any significant change in the exchange rate at the time of delivery.

Finally, you should also take into account logistical issues such as Customs duties, taxes, tariffs, and added shipping costs due to incomplete trade documentation.

The following are some questions you may want to consider answering or using in a checklist as part of your due diligence prior to performing a sourcing analysis for services:

Questions for Sourcing Services

- How are the services configured or packaged?
- What is the breakdown of tasks involved with the service?
- What are the typical qualifications of people who are providing these services?
- Are there benchmarks readily used through the marketplace for this service?
- What methods are used to measure/evaluate the service?
- How are the services supported? Does the company have customer service?

Standards, Service Levels, and Benchmarks

- Do performance standards or performance measures exist in this market segment?
- How is quality assurance and acceptance managed: by the buyer, the seller, or both?

Pricing and Market Conditions

- Are there cost differences for different quality service levels?
- What are the market prices for this service?
- What are the historical market trends concerning quality, performance, and price?
- What is the usual amount of risk for this type of service?
- What is the extent of competition in this service segment?

Operations

- Are performance incentives used? What kinds: monetary and/or non-monetary?

- What is the environment in which the service is performed?
- Are there people or computer interfaces that must be considered?
- How long has this management service team been in place?
- Is commercial financing customary? Are discounts offered?
- What are the industry standards for insuring, licensing, or bonding service providers?

Organizing Information

Once we have completed the process of gathering information, we will want to organize it and put it into an operational mode for execution. Most often, the results of our research will be consolidated into a weighted decision matrix that will enable us to prequalify the most capable suppliers so that we can include them on our bid list or short supplier list for negotiation.

It is probably best to organize the information in the same categories that you used for research. Doing so will enable you to compare each supplier to the others in all the major categories we outlined earlier. The output will enable sound decision making.

- **Financial and business metrics.** Key measures of financial health and sustainability
- **Technology.** The nature of the technology used in its operations and its output as well as patents and other intellectual property
- **Manufacturing and distribution.** Important elements include the age of equipment, location of facilities, capacity utilization, and methods of distribution
- **Governance.** Decision-making processes and legal relationships
- **Business relationships and country risks.** Consider partners, suppliers, employees, and the community

Assessing Potential Suppliers' Capabilities

How are we going to use the information we have now gathered and organized?

- We will use it to develop competition between suppliers that will lead to meeting our interests in achieving overall value.
- The knowledge gained will provide a better understanding of the drivers in that particular product or service (and industry), enabling us to develop strategies for managing supplier performance.
- The data will help us assess the risks that will require monitoring in the future.

- We can use this information to enable our understanding of the suppliers' motivation points, providing the basis for a high-quality negotiation plan.
- It will help us align the needs of our supplier with our requirements for a stronger relationship.
- It will provide us with a holistic and realistic approach to overcoming the obstacles and leveraging the value opportunities inherent in the sourcing process.

Figure 5.1 shows the basic types of information exchanged between the buying organization and the supplying organizations, or the type of information you might try to obtain from available third-party data. The basis of the research will be along the lines shown as Buying Company output, such as the physical characteristics and functional descriptions that often accompany published specifications. The returning input from suppliers will be product data, such as performance, measurements, warranties, and so on, along with industry data, market structure and general selling terms, and data about the individual supplier needed to support source selection.

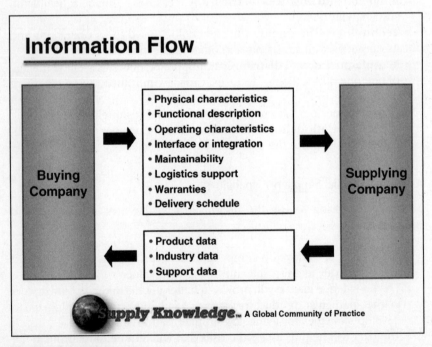

FIGURE 5.1 Information Flow

As you formulate the list of information that you need, keep in mind that the output provided by the supplying organization is to a large degree dependent on the information requested by the buying organization. The seller may not be aware of the nuances of your specific needs or requirements.

eSourcing Tools

There is so much information available on the Internet that sourcing professionals can easily face information overload. However, when used appropriately, eSourcing tools can expedite the gathering of information, since it's virtually all in the same place.

In choosing a particular item for a one-time purchase, eSourcing also helps us decide which product will best serve our requirement(s). The side-by-side comparison is a popular way to show a comparative analysis, especially where commercial products are being researched and technical specifications are available. These comparison tools are included in most Web catalog sites.

Conducting Market Analysis

Market analysis is an important tool for gathering information about pricing and availability trends, inherent risks in a particular industry, and the structure of the market itself: what its drivers and critical barriers are. We can learn what new and existing technology is available and assess its suitability; we can learn who the key suppliers are and what advantages they offer.

Market analysis can become an extensive and time-consuming project, so you will need to adjust the amount of time spent according to the urgency of the requirement. An urgent requirement just may not allow the time required to properly research the market. Review the estimated price of the acquisition, where low-price purchases do not merit extensive research. Be sure to consider the complexity of the requirement, where more or less time must be spent in fact finding and analysis for highly complex acquisitions.

Analyzing the Market

One of the primary objectives of market analysis is to develop an awareness of the opportunities and threats evolving in the particular market. David A. Aaker, currently professor emeritus at the Haas School of Business of the University of California, Berkeley, outlines the major categories of market analysis:

- Market size (current and future)
- Market growth rate
- Market profitability
- Industry cost structure
- Distribution channels
- Market trends
- Key success factors

MARKET SIZE We generally relate market size to the total dollar value of aggregated sales. Market share is important when assessing a particular supplier's position within that market. This information is typically available through Department of Labor/Department of Commerce publications, although it is not always as current as we might like it. We can also find information through trade magazines and trade associations as well as research firms specializing in that particular economic market segment.

MARKET GROWTH RATE The rate of growth in any particular market segment will tell you if there will be market capacity available and for how long. This information is usually garnered from the same sites noted earlier, although in some cases you may have to project the information into the future yourself in order to utilize it fully. There are a number of forecasting and statistical techniques available for doing this; most easily used is linear regression analysis, which plots a straight line from the past into some future date using a formula found in most spreadsheet programs.

MARKET PROFITABILITY If companies in a particular market are profitable, they are more likely to provide a relatively stable source of supply. Many factors influence profit, including the balance of supply and demand, the ease with which new firms can enter the market, the competitive nature of the market, and who (buyer or supplier) holds the most power.

INDUSTRY COST STRUCTURE We can use our knowledge of the market's cost structure to identify current and emerging opportunities for leverage and negotiation planning purposes. In a competitive market with relatively inflexible cost elements, pricing will be able to fluctuate only within a relatively narrow range to maintain profitability (under most circumstances).

DISTRIBUTION CHANNELS How are customer orders generated and fulfilled? The more hands a product passes through, the higher its price and the slower its delivery tend to be. A shorter pipeline or supply chain generally ensures faster response times with less inventory and thus less cost.

MARKET TRENDS Fluctuations in price and availability are common in all markets. Supply and demand vary and affect prices depending on the complexity of the supply chain. Understanding these fluctuations and being able to forecast them to some extent can result in buying opportunities that lower cost.

KEY SUCCESS FACTORS Advanced technology, higher quality and satisfaction levels, and economies of scale are just some of the factors for success within a given market. First to market and access to distribution resources provide individual companies within the market more opportunity for success.

Determining Changing Marketplace Factors

One of the most significant determinants of sourcing decisions generates from the nature of changes in the marketplace. Supply and demand continually interact to produce varying pricing profiles. When product is in short supply or production resources come under threat (e.g., oil and the Middle East), prices can rise dramatically, and capacity limits may create supply allocations. Organizations wishing to continually work with the most price-competitive suppliers who stay up to date on the latest technological advances and business methods must maintain an aggressive review process that periodically surveys the market as conditions change.

ECONOMIC CONDITIONS Supply and demand forces continually drive prices up and down. As economic conditions change, demand increases or declines, generating shortages or excesses in supply at any given time. As previously noted, increased supply or decreased demand (or combinations of both) generally lead to reduced prices. What drives these fluctuations can be a mystery. However, the astute procurement professional can take advantage of these conditions by seeking increased competition during periods of abundant supply and declining prices when suppliers are more anxious to seek new business or, conversely, by locking in prices through contracts when facing periods of shortage or inflationary pricing.

MARKET COMPLEXITY The extent to which an organization's economic strategy can be employed—for example, when to lock in prices through extended contracts or when to pay more for higher quality levels—depends somewhat significantly on the complexity of the market. Markets with few suppliers and little potential for product substitution tend to offer only limited opportunities for you to use competition to your advantage. However, in markets in which widely competitive forces exist, shortages in one product can be easily offset by substituting another—that is, markets with greater complexity provide the buyer with more leverage to gain pricing improvements. Cost reduction efforts can produce the greatest results in industries with broadly diverse alternatives, so the sourcing effort should always begin by determining the nature of the marketplace.

NATURE OF COMPETITION   The nature of competition in any particular market varies. Are there many technical solutions available, or only one or two? Is the market characterized by geographical limitations with very high transportation costs? If, for example, the product being purchased is covered by a patent or controlled by patented manufacturing technology, competition will be unlikely. Similarly, when start-up costs are high, such as those that occur in the development of proprietary tooling, competition tends to become constricted once the initial sourcing decision is made. It is always wise to understand the nature of competition in this regard before committing to generating short-term cost reductions since the sourcing effort will likely require major engineering efforts.

When dealing with sources of critical supplies or services, the buying organization needs to maintain continual vigilance for potential traps that will unknowingly limit the nature of the competition for that particular product or service. You must also develop strategies for dealing with such risks in the future.

ANALYSIS OF TECHNOLOGICAL TRENDS   When technological change drives conditions in the marketplace, new sources of supply must always be under consideration. New technology frequently generates new opportunities for capital investment, and emerging businesses tend to spring up everywhere. The buyer should be sensitive to these opportunities but be able to balance them with the need for maintaining long-term relationships that produce value beyond price or the latest fad in technology.

With critical supplies and services, one should always monitor the supply base to ensure that existing sources are keeping abreast of technology and adding improvements as necessary. Suppliers that do not constantly upgrade their processes to take advantage of new technology could easily become obsolete. The buyer should consider ways to continually monitor existing suppliers and their technological position relative to their competitor so that ongoing changes do not adversely affect their organization's own competitive position.

PERFORMANCE   As economic conditions change, so can supplier performance. Suppliers under continual pricing pressures due to emerging global markets, for example, may tend to sacrifice some of the quality that qualified them for your business in the first place. Delivery delays, cuts in services, and quality failures are often the early signs of declining performance due to economic hardship. Companies providing critical supplies and services need to be continually measured against industry performance standards. Initial signs of deteriorating performance should be met with clear improvement projects and, depending on the rapidity of decline, additional sourcing activities.

Summary

In this chapter, we examined two major concepts related to sourcing: supplier research and market analysis. We began with an overview of supplier research methods and techniques and how research is conducted. This included a number of major sources of information, such as experts, trade associations, government agencies, directories, and consultants. Then we examined what information was important and what questions need to be answered in each of the major evaluation categories, including how best to organize the information. Turning next to market analysis, we examined the most important elements to consider and how we assess the changing marketplace. We concluded with a discussion of the nature of economic conditions and the analysis of technological trends.

CHAPTER **6**

Solicitation of Bids and Proposals

The next step in the sourcing process is the solicitation phase. Solicitation, in simple terms, is the process of requesting bids or proposals from potential suppliers. Once the supplier research and market analysis is complete, and we have identified several suppliers that are well positioned in their markets and appear to have the qualifications we need, the sourcing team can develop a solicitation plan. The plan should establish the method to be used for the solicitation and, when applicable, the type of contract to be used.

In this chapter, we examine the solicitation plan and the methods of solicitation.

Solicitation Planning

To a large degree, the solicitation plan is driven by the nature of what is being acquired and the makeup of the supply base in the particular market in which we are sourcing. In the process of developing the plan, we must evaluate the nature of the acquisition as a way of narrowing the sourcing possibilities. Keep in mind that there are sourcing and procurement actions that fall outside the requirement for solicitation, such as purchasing card transactions and spot or micropurchases that may simply be "shopped" by the procurement group.

Product or Service Characteristics

In Chapter 6, we noted that the goods and services we typically source will have one of three possible general characteristics, determined by the Statement of Work (SOW) or specification and the nature of the market we discover during the market analysis phase. We based this division on the Federal Acquisition Regulations (FAR), which outline the three main categories of product. The product categories outlined in the FAR can be applied to commercial sourcing as well. For simplicity, we have included services and provided a bit of paraphrasing for each category to help keep it simple.

1. The product or service is commercially available, meaning that it can be purchased by the general public in its present form. Another way of saying this is that the product or service is available off the shelf.
2. The product or service is commercially available but will need some modification to meet our requirements or specifications. An example of this would be a field generator requiring balloon tires so that it can be towed through a sandy or swampy area; the generator is standard but the tires will have to be sourced separately.
3. There is no commercially available product or service that can be used to meet our requirements; we will require one that is fully customized to meet the specific need.

Here's why we simplified our definitions. This is the official U.S. government's definition of a commercial item, as specified in FAR Part 2—Definitions of Words and Terms, Subpart 2.1—Definitions:

"Commercial item" means—

(1) Any item, other than real property, that is of a type customarily used by the general public or by non-governmental entities for purposes other than governmental purposes, and—

(i) Has been sold, leased, or licensed to the general public; or

(ii) Has been offered for sale, lease, or license to the general public;

(2) Any item that evolved from an item described in paragraph (1) of this definition through advances in technology or performance and that is not yet available in the commercial marketplace, but will be available in the commercial marketplace in time to satisfy the delivery requirements under a Government solicitation;

(3) Any item that would satisfy a criterion expressed in paragraphs (1) or (2) of this definition, but for—

(i) Modifications of a type customarily available in the commercial marketplace; or

(ii) Minor modifications of a type not customarily available in the commercial marketplace made to meet Federal Government requirements. Minor modifications means modifications that do not significantly alter the nongovernmental function or essential physical characteristics of an item or component, or change the purpose of a process. Factors to be considered in determining whether a modification is minor include the value and size of the modification and the comparative value and size of the final product. Dollar values and percentages may be used as guideposts, but are not conclusive evidence that a modification is minor;

(4) Any combination of items meeting the requirements of paragraphs (1), (2), (3), or (5) of this definition that are of a type customarily combined and sold in combination to the general public;

(5) Installation services, maintenance services, repair services, training services, and other services if—

   (i) Such services are procured for support of an item referred to in paragraph (1), (2), (3), or (4) of this definition, regardless of whether such services are provided by the same source or at the same time as the item; and

   (ii) The source of such services provides similar services contemporaneously to the general public under terms and conditions similar to those offered to the Federal Government;

(6) Services of a type offered and sold competitively in substantial quantities in the commercial marketplace based on established catalog or market prices for specific tasks performed or specific outcomes to be achieved and under standard commercial terms and conditions. For purposes of these services—

   (i) "Catalog price" means a price included in a catalog, price list, schedule, or other form that is regularly maintained by the manufacturer or vendor, is either published or otherwise available for inspection by customers, and states prices at which sales are currently, or were last, made to a significant number of buyers constituting the general public; and

(continued)

(continued)

> *(ii) "Market prices" means current prices that are estab-*
> *lished in the course of ordinary trade between buyers*
> *and sellers free to bargain and that can be substanti-*
> *ated through competition or from sources independent*
> *of the offerors.*
> *(7) Any item, combination of items, or service referred to in*
> *paragraphs (1) through (6) of this definition, notwithstand-*
> *ing the fact that the item, combination of items, or service*
> *is transferred between or among separate divisions, sub-*
> *sidiaries, or affiliates of a contractor; or*
> *(8) A nondevelopmental item, if the procuring agency deter-*
> *mines the item was developed exclusively at private expense*
> *and sold in substantial quantities, on a competitive basis,*
> *to multiple State and local governments.*

> *"Commercially available off-the-shelf (COTS)" item—*

> *(1) Means any item of supply (including construction material)*
> *that is—*
> > *(i) A commercial item (as defined in paragraph (1) of the*
> > *definition in this section);*
> > *(ii) Sold in substantial quantities in the commercial mar-*
> > *ketplace; and*
> > *(iii) Offered to the Government, under a contract or sub-*
> > *contract at any tier, without modification, in the same*
> > *form in which it is sold in the commercial marketplace;*
> > *and*
> *(2) Does not include bulk cargo, as defined in section 3 of*
> *the Shipping Act of 1984 (46 U.S.C. App. 1702), such as*
> *agricultural products and petroleum products.*

A fourth option that we generally exclude from these categories is the acquisition of professional services, such as engineering or consulting. We address these services separately at the end of this section.

Solicitation Types

Each of the characteristics or categories outlined leads to a somewhat different set of solicitation possibilities, although in some cases the same method can be used in more than one category.

COMMERCIALLY AVAILABLE PRODUCT/SERVICE Products and services that are off the shelf share the same characteristics and are, for the most part, interchangeable if there is more than one supplying producer. As a result, the acquisition decisions will focus on elements such as pricing, terms and conditions, availability, return policy, and so on.

In a competitive market, we have several viable options for solicitation:

- The *Invitation for Bid (IFB)* is used by government procurement, usually for requirements over $25,000. The bidder responds with a sealed bid to be opened publicly at a stated date and time. It is primarily a price competition and the lowest bid will win.
- The *Request for Quotation (RFQ)* is used by both government (usually under $25,000) and commercial organizations. The RFQ simply requests a quotation for price and delivery where other terms are already specified, as in the case where Master Supply Agreements or Master Service Agreements are in place. (The acronym "RFQ" is sometimes used to mean "Request for Qualification," a request similar to the Request for Information, or RFI.)
- A *reverse auction* enables suppliers to bid against one another in a real-time bidding event. Bidders are blind to one another, but everyone can see the current lowest bid price. The auction is typically hosted by a third party, although there are a number of software systems that enable buyers to work directly with suppliers. Here again, terms and conditions are already specified so the lowest price wins the business.
- *Competitive negotiations* are held with suppliers whose bids are the most favorable. It is a process that is rarely used for simple acquisitions, since negotiations typically follow the suppliers' submission of bids and can have the undesirable effect of suppliers "padding" future bids to enable the buyer to negotiate back to its intended pricing.

If goods or nonprofessional services are being procured, negotiations are conducted with each of the favored providers. Price is important but need not be the only factor in the negotiation. After negotiations have been conducted with each supplier, the sourcing team recommends the one that offers the best value.

In a noncompetitive market for commercial goods or services, one characterized by a sole source (only one supplier in existence), there is no option for competitive bidding. As a result, there must be some form of negotiation if we intend to achieve lower costs or improved business terms. Many sole-source suppliers, however, are not inclined to negotiate. Since they have a legal monopoly, there is little we can do in this regard during sourcing operations. We do, however, submit a RFQ in most cases, unless there is a published price covering our volume.

In the case of a single source, where the market is competitive but we choose to use only one supplier, there are often more options available than with a sole source. But if the decision has already been made to use a particular supplier, competitive bidding would be unethical since there is no chance of an award going to a different supplier. We do issue an RFQ and conduct negotiations though, unless we have an existing Master Agreement that already covers the common element for which we would typically negotiate. We address negotiation strategies for single-source acquisitions in Chapter 8.

COMMERCIALLY AVAILABLE PRODUCT/SERVICE REQUIRING MODIFICATION   In a situation where we require a nonstandard modification made to an existing commercial item, we likely have the same options as we have with a commercial item. But unless we have a precise specification for our requirement, we also have the option of using a Request for Proposal (RFP) where there is competition in the market.

REQUEST FOR PROPOSAL   The RFP is used primarily to solicit proposals for services. Since services are generally tailored to the organization's special needs, the Statement of Work becomes the focal point document. However, where modification is required to a product to meet some specific requirement and we have no particular solution in mind, an RFP should be used to solicit proposed solutions to the modification.

The RFP generally follows a standard format that contains the Statement of Work or some similar expression of need.

An RFP is often composed from existing data for the requirements or SOW/specification. It typically consists of three sections: The first can be called an Introduction since it describes your organization and the purpose of the RFP. This is followed by the Requirements section which can range from a simple compilation of existing known information and a description of likely needs, across the spectrum to a fully detailed Statement of Work. The requirements section will then be followed by the Attachments (or Addendums) section listing existing information or describing previous history.

The RFP often provides a framework that you can use to compare proposed solutions and evaluate proposals and to help you and your team select the most qualified source.

You can also use RFP responses to develop an SOW (where none exists), by combining proposals from several suppliers, selecting the most appropriate elements from each. In this case, you would then perform a two-step bidding process and follow the suppliers' RFP submissions with your own specification in an RFQ.

The RFP can also be used as a means of preparing the way for the actual contract formation. You will want to include a copy of your organization's standard terms and conditions and ask the supplier to determine if they are acceptable. Or you may want to get even more specific, for example, and include a requirement for payment terms of Net "X" days. Then, based on the responses you receive, you will be able to determine if there are suppliers willing to meet those terms.

Throughout the process, you will have the opportunity to get to know some of the supplier's staff that you will likely be working with once you award the contract. It is important to use these opportunities to build collaborative rather than adversarial relationships that will serve both organizations, reducing the ramp-up time once the contract has been signed. A summary of the three sections of the RFP follows.

1. **Introduction.** The introductory section contains general information about your company that will help prospective suppliers better gauge your needs. It also clearly states the problem or situation that gives rise to the requirements and what the current status is. In providing useful information about your organization, you might consider elements such as years in business, gross revenue, profitability, employee count, product lines, market share (for main products or services), and number of customers (and notable customers and locations of operation).

   It is important to be factual and, at the same time, use this introduction as an opportunity to present your organization in its most favorable light. The responding supplier will most often have to expend some significant effort in answering your request, so this information might be helpful in making its decision to respond or not.

   The introductory section also outlines some of the requirements for response submission including deadlines, timelines if multiple stages of fact finding and proposal are being considered, along with any legal disclaimers that may be appropriate. One commonly used disclaimer reserves the rights of your organization to make an award or not to award at all, as it so chooses. Often this section includes any supplemental material required from the supplier, such as the requirement to provide references from other customers.

   It is often productive to advise a potential bidder of the evaluation criteria without being overly specific. For instance, you might include a statement to the effect that a suitable technical solution is critical to the project and will be the primary consideration for an award, followed, let's say, by pricing and proven track record.

2. **Requirements.** The requirements section typically consists of a statement of need, which describes in detail the specific objectives of the purchase. This statement is almost always prepared by the using

department since it is the group with the proper expertise. However, since the procurement group is responsible for making the supplier selection and the award, you should become familiar with these requirements.

In the requirements section, you want to ensure that all the known details regarding the work to be performed have been included. Details most likely include elements such as time requirements and operational frequency, known constraints, quality requirements, and elements that will be measured. One way to do this is by creating a Work Breakdown Structure that lists each of the deliverables required.

To the extent possible, group the criteria in a logical context that follows some easily understood format and insist that the supplier respond in that format. This way you won't have to chase through several unformatted responses to dig out the information you need.

In stating the requirements, avoid establishing restrictive criteria that are out of alignment with current industry practices; this is another good reason for you to research the market prior to issuing the RFP. Be aware that the requirements do not generate a sole-source selection situation, where only one supplier is capable of fulfilling the requirements.

3. **Attachments.** The attachments section commonly includes boilerplate terms and conditions and other contractual requirements. If available, include a copy of a standard contract so that the supplier has a chance to determine if any issues might develop during the contract formation phase. Often the RFP contains a request to indicate whether these are acceptable terms and conditions and, if not, where there are potential areas for negotiation.

If you have a response template, include one for the supplier to use to submit its response. Providing a sample service-level metric so that the supplier understands the level of detail you will be evaluating is also useful.

NO COMMERCIAL ITEM AVAILABLE: REQUIRES CUSTOMIZATION   Sourcing (and soliciting proposals) for a product or service that does not yet exist is always challenging. How do you know where to start? Well, it may take a bit more work, but for a customized *product*, sourcing really is not that difficult. In fact, virtually all industries have numerous suppliers that specialize in providing customization. For companies that have the resources and facilities to accommodate custom-built products—we often refer to these specialists as "job shops"—it can be a profitable business. As a general rule, where there is profit, there is competition.

Some industries are actually built around custom products. Injection molding (and its accompanying tool making), application-specific integrated circuits, and metal stamping, just to mention a few, serve the custom need for producing specialized components in practically all industries.

Where technical specifications and drawings exist, the solicitation is straightforward. We would use a typical sourcing process. Once potential suppliers are identified and prequalified, we can use an RFQ, conduct a reverse auction, or engage in competitive negotiations, as outlined earlier.

Where no specifications exist, just a concept, we would use an RFP, following the guidelines provided earlier. Once the proposals are in, we may consider a two-step process where we develop the specifications from the supplier proposals or even competitive negotiations. And certainly do not rule out the reverse auction, although in most cases such a method can take more effort and produce marginal results.

Customized *services* must be handled somewhat differently. With services, supplier prequalification during the sourcing process can require a great deal of extra effort. Outsourcing a customer service function or an information technology operation that is organization specific, for example, requires far more due diligence simply because there are significantly more elements involved in the qualification process. Customized services usually begin with extensive supplier contact, to determine how the supplier "fits" with our organization. Often there are formal preproposal briefings to flesh out the requirements so that suppliers can get a fuller picture of what is needed. Typically, in such cases, the entire acquisition process is conducted by a cross-functional team and formally managed as a project.

The solicitation mechanism for customized services always requires an RFP. Because each supplier's proposal is going to be different, and sometimes radically so, supplier selection may require additional steps. Here we can use a two-step sourcing process. We can also use a process developed by the federal government called "competitive discussions." Discussions are not negotiations (and this should be made very clear to suppliers) and so require a greater degree of collaboration. Included in these discussions will be a good deal of fact finding and questioning regarding proposed solutions, along with staffing, timing, and service levels. The purpose is to gain a better understanding of the supplier's position and capabilities. The end product should be a clearer assessment of each proposer's strengths and weaknesses.

We can follow the proposal (or secondary bid process) and competitive discussions with negotiations, by soliciting improvements in areas where a particular supplier's proposal is weak. Our RFP should clearly state that we are under no obligation to accept a proposal on face value and that we may not even make an award as a result of the process.

REQUEST FOR INFORMATION   The RFI is a tool used in sourcing to help determine a supplier's capabilities and financial health. Our experience shows

TABLE 6.1 Types of Solicitations and Where Used

Product/Service Type	Competitive Market	Noncompetitive Market
Commercial	IFB, RFQ, RFI, sealed bid	RFQ
Commercial with modification	IFB, RFP, RFI, sealed bid	RFP
Customized	IFB, RFP, RFI, sealed bid	RFP

that most responses to an RFI by suppliers tend to become sales pitches. However, using an RFI is more relevant to the sourcing process itself than to the actual solicitation so perhaps these sales pitches are not inappropriate. Keep in mind that the RFI is a formal process that can actually become part of the contracting process to the same extent a supplier's quote or proposal may contain legally binding elements. It must be handled equitably, with the same request provided to all potential suppliers, and any clarifications made to one participant must be passed on to all.

SEALED BID   Any RFQ, RFP, or IFB can call for a sealed bid, depending on the nature of the acquisition and the market. A sealed bid is one that is not opened until a specific date and time and, for the most part, the opening is conducted publicly. It is not a solicitation process in itself; rather, it is a method of response to a solicitation. Sealed bids are used primarily in high-value government contracts to maintain the confidentiality of the bids (and the bidder) and to ensure an equitable award to the lowest bidder.

Table 6.1 provides a summary of solicitation types.

Solicitation Methods

Now that we have an understanding of the types of solicitations we can use, let's turn our attention to the methods we can use to deploy them. Essentially, we will examine the communication tools available for distributing and responding to the RFQ, IFB, and RFP.

Mail or Courier

Possibly the simplest means for distribution is the traditional method of mailing or distribution by couriers such as FedEx or UPS. The only issues that typically arise from this method are ensuring that the request gets to the right individual and the answers get back to the originator. It is also a comparatively slow method when compared with the tools available in the electronic age.

Published Posting

In this method, an "expression of interest" is solicited through newspaper ads or through industry and government publications. An interested supplier follows the instructions for getting detailed requirements and bid documents from the buyer. This method is not in widespread use today and is found mostly in cases where it is required by law.

Web-Based Portals

Web-based portals are buyer or collaborative group web sites that serve the area of solicitation primarily as static tools for distributing solicitations in any format to the supply base. Generally they are maintained by the buying organization, but there has been increasing movement toward consolidated sites that have developed relationships with communities of suppliers and communities of buyers. They are used to prepare and publish electronic solicitations to participating suppliers and, sometimes, accept their responses. Very often, this service also includes a range of software tools that are subscribed to as Software as a Service (SAAS).

An early example of a Web-based industry portal is Covisint, which began operation in the 1990s as a means for the auto industry to collaborate with its suppliers and has subsequently expanded into a number of other industries. Surprisingly, it is still in operation. Other early consolidators providing sourcing, solicitation, and collaboration tools include Sciquest (for the biotech and pharmaceutical industries), Ariba (one of the first to provide SAAS for its customers), Oracle, and SAP, just to mention a few. Most Fortune 500 companies—Intel, Cisco, HP, Procter & Gamble, and so on—maintain their own supplier portals.

E-Mail Solicitations

Instead of using postal mail or couriers, solicitations are often sent directly to the supplier's sales contact by e-mail. Other than the method of distribution and response, the e-mail solicitation is handled in exactly the same manner as any other type of solicitation; the method leverages commonly used technology to reduce the cost and time required by older methods.

The only potential issue with using e-mail for the solicitation process is the maintenance of security to ensure that confidentiality is not violated and that the information in any documents is not compromised.

Telephone

For simple or low-cost acquisitions and for acquisitions competitively bid among suppliers with Master Agreements in place, a telephone solicitation may be appropriate. Here we typically adopt the format of a typical RFQ, for a known item. There are some caveats, however:

- It is recommended that the individual conducting the solicitation operate from a script to ensure that all competitors receive exactly the same information.
- If any questions arise that might affect the bid, all of those solicited must be notified of the question and its response, as in any formal process.
- Keep good documentation of whom you spoke with, when the conversation took place, and the exact bid that was received.
- In the interest of ethical behavior, never reveal the bids of other suppliers (or even who they are) in any form, and never coach a bidder to provide a quote lower than the others.
- Confirm the accepted bid in writing.

Mailing Lists

Many organizations maintain an extensive bidders' list of companies that have a previous history with the sourcing organization or have responded well to earlier solicitations. Often this list can be used in place of extensive market research and prequalification processes so that the sourcing individual has only to conduct a brief survey of the market to determine current conditions and if any significant changes have occurred in the supply base. All other elements of a standard solicitation would apply.

Crowdsourcing

Crowdsourcing is a relatively new and increasingly popular avenue for sourcing and solicitation of relatively simple services. It is a method that also leverages current technology.

In its basic form, crowdsourcing works through posting a set of requirements on a specialized job board. Members with access to the site (which is usually open to the public) can offer bids using a simplified online form by responding with their prices, lead times, and credentials. These bids are often sealed to the extent that they can be seen only by the buyer.

On many sites, members are given a page to include their qualifications and references, along with feedback from previous customers. This method is proving to be a viable tool for freelancers in service areas such as web site development, simple programming, writing, graphic design, marketing collateral, and various administrative support jobs. One of the more interesting aspects of this process is that responses can come from anywhere in the world, since virtually all of the work can be conducted remotely.

FIGURE 6.1 The Elance Job Site

Source: Copyright © 1999–2010 Elance, Inc. All Rights Reserved. Elance is the registered service mark of Elance, Inc.

Some of the sites that are available include Amazon's Mechanical Turk with its proprietary system called HITs, for *Human Intelligence Tasks*, individual tasks that can be worked on remotely. Another system that has been in existence since late in the last century is Elance, specializing in a narrower form of crowdsourcing focused on categories of expertise (as shown in Figure 6.1). Others include Sologig.com, Guru.com, and Freelancer.com— and this is just a partial list.

Summary

This chapter focused on the types and methods of solicitation. We began with an overview of solicitation planning, describing the product or service categories and characteristics as we see them. We examined the three categories: commercially available product/service, commercially available product/service requiring modification, and no commercially available product/service that requires complete customization. We then went over the various solicitation methods in use today, such as postal mail or courier, publication posting, Web-based portals, e-mail, telephone, mailing lists, and the latest method, crowdsourcing.

CHAPTER 7

Supplier Evaluation and Selection

In this chapter, we examine many of the criteria and methods available for evaluating and selecting key suppliers.

From a sourcing perspective, supplier evaluation and selection is one of the more critical activities in strategic sourcing planning. To a large extent, an organization is empowered in its capability to execute on its planning by the strength of its supply base. Conversely, it is limited by its suppliers' inability to meet commitments.

There are a number of circumstances in which we need to carefully evaluate suppliers in some detail. Most commonly, a formal evaluation and qualification process will be used when we are selecting a supplier for a complex or high-cost one-time contract or when we are establishing a partnering relationship that will include a Master Supply or Master Service Agreement that may extend for several years.

Evaluation Criteria

How we choose a particular supplier is largely dependent on the criteria we use for evaluation and how we apply these metrics. There is a vast pool of criteria to choose from, but not all are equally valuable in any given situation so they must be chosen carefully and with our objectives clearly in sight. Evaluation metrics also have a dual function since they will be used later to evaluate the supplier's ongoing "scorecard" performance; this is another reason to make careful choices early in the sourcing process.

Comparative Evaluation: Business Criteria

There are two major categories to consider in the supplier evaluation process: business criteria and technical criteria. We can describe business criteria, which we discuss first, as those elements that evaluate the health and performance of an organization and will help predict how well a particular supplier can meet its contractual obligations over time.

HISTORICAL DATA   Often we can turn to the past as a predictor of the future. We can ask: How well did the supplier meet its obligations to its customers in the past? But this is not a general question, and we need to develop a specific set of evaluation criteria based on our own current needs. If we have past experience with the particular supplier we are evaluating, we can use information from our files to assist; if not, we will have to turn to other sources, sometimes the supplier itself, to get the data we need to conduct our evaluation. Some of the categories we will want to examine are included in the next sections.

FINANCIAL ANALYSIS   In the modern global sourcing environment, it has become increasingly important to perform financial analysis in order to assess overall supply base risk factors. Financial analysis demonstrates a sound fiduciary responsibility to shareholders and may be required in order to meet audit compliance requirements.

When we refer to financial analysis tools, we typically mean the methods used to analyze the financial performance of an organization or a particular activity within the organization. These methods are often expressed in terms of a specific financial ratio. Presented in this section are some of the more common measures you should have the ability to analyze and understand.

In sourcing, we use financial ratios both internally for gauging our own organization's performance and externally for assessing the performance of suppliers. Often these measures help select or qualify suppliers on the basis of their financial strength, competitive advantage, and financial leverage.

To properly evaluate individual financial ratios, it is important that you view them with respect to the historical performance of the supplier or the ratios of similar firms in the industry. Ratios must be viewed as indicators rather than absolutes, so a proper evaluation will require comparison of a set of values, rather than just one or two. Keep in mind that ratios are dependent on the Generally Accepted Accounting Principles used, which may vary somewhat based on how the company chooses to present its data. Such financial data should be considered a snapshot of a period in time, so it's important to view financial trends rather than individual measurements.

MEASURES OF LIQUIDITY   Liquidity ratios indicate an organization's ability to meet short-term financial obligations. Since they are of special interest to credit organizations, they may reflect the organization's ability to borrow funds to meet the shortfall in its current time horizon.

Current Ratio   The Current Ratio tells you whether an organization is able to meet its current financial obligations. It measures an organization's ability to meet short-term debt obligations; the higher the ratio, the more liquid the organization is from a cash flow perspective.

The Current Ratio is calculated by dividing current assets by current liabilities. Current assets are those that can be converted to cash within a year; typically they include cash, marketable securities, inventory, and accounts receivable. Current liabilities are those that are due within a year; typically accounts payable, accrued salaries and wages, outstanding lines of credit, and the principal of long-term loans.

The standard Current Ratio for a healthy business is 2.0, meaning it has twice as many assets as liabilities.

Quick Ratio   Very closely related to Current Ratio, the Quick Ratio measures an organization's ability to fund its short-term financial obligations through its most liquid assets. It is also called the acid test.

The Quick Ratio is calculated by taking current assets *less inventories*, divided by current liabilities.

A low Quick Ratio (below 0.5) indicates that an organization may be slow in paying its obligations. A Quick Ratio of 2.0 or more is desirable.

Receivables Turnover Ratio   The Receivables Turnover Ratio calculates how many days it takes the organization to receive payment from its customers.

Receivables turnover is calculated by dividing net sales (in dollars) by receivables.

The faster accounts receivable are converted to cash, the greater the ability of the organization to meet its current liabilities.

Payables Turnover Ratio   The Payables Turnover Ratio indicates how long it takes, on average, for an organization to pay its bills. It is a calculation of how often payables turn over during the year.

It is calculated by dividing the cost of goods sold by payables.

A high ratio means there is a relatively short time between purchase of goods and services and payment for them. A low ratio may be a sign that the company has chronic cash shortages.

Debt-to-Equity Ratio   The Debt-to-Equity Ratio indicates how much the company is leveraged (in debt) by comparing what is owed to what is owned. Equity and debt are two key figures on a financial statement, so lenders or investors often use the relationship of these two figures to evaluate risk. The ratio of an organization's equity to its long-term debt provides a window into how strong its finances are.

Equity will include goods and property, plus any claims it has against other entities. Debts will include both current and long-term liabilities.

Debt to Equity is calculated by dividing total liabilities by total equity.

A high Debt-to-Equity Ratio could indicate that the company may be overleveraged.

MEASURES OF PROFITABILITY   Profitability ratios are used to determine if adequate profits are being generated based on the investments made in the corporation. Profitability reflects the organization's ability to generate enough income to maintain its financial health and growth in both the near term and long term.

Gross Profit Margin Ratio   The Gross Profit Margin Ratio indicates how efficiently a business is using its materials and labor in the production process. It shows the percentage of net sales remaining after subtracting cost of goods sold. A high gross profit margin indicates that a business can make a reasonable profit on sales, as long as it keeps overhead costs in control.

It is calculated by dividing gross profit by total sales.

Net Operating Margin   Net Operating Margin (NOM) reflects the profitability of the organization by calculating the percentage of its *total operating income* (sales less direct costs) to its overall sales:

$$NOM = \text{Net Operating Income} \div \text{Revenue}$$

Return on Assets Ratio   The Return on Assets (ROA) calculation shows how effective an organization is at using its assets. The ROA is a test of capital utilization—how much profit (before interest and income tax) a business earned on the total capital used to make that profit.

ROA is an indicator of an organization's profitability

It is calculated by dividing Earnings Before Interest and Taxes (EBIT) by Net Operating Assets.

$$ROA = \text{Net Income (EBIT)} \div \text{Average Assets for the Period}$$

Return on Total Assets/Return on Net Assets   Return on Total Assets (ROTA) and Return on Net Assets (RONA) are measures used to determine how effectively capital is deployed within the organization. Here net income (i.e., revenue less expenses) is divided by the value of assets in operation to determine effectiveness:

$$ROTA = \text{Net Income} \div \text{Total Assets}$$

Return on Investment   Return on Investment (ROI) describes the effectiveness of a particular investment in terms of how long it takes to recover (or earn back) the initial funding. ROI can be calculated as the *Net Present Value (NPV)* of the revenue created divided by the initial investment:

$$ROI = (Savings \times Time) - (Discount\ Rate \times Time)$$

Financial Data Sources   Some useful information sources include:

- Dun & Bradstreet: www.dnb.com
- EDGAR: www.sec.gov
- Hoovers: www.hoovers.com
- MarketWatch: www.marketwatch.com
- Moody's: www.moodys.com
- Standard & Poor's: www.standardandpoors.com

MEASURES OF EFFICIENCY   Organizations operating at high to maximum efficiency levels can increase the capacity of their business and thereby leverage their capabilities to operate at minimum cost. Often this translates into lower prices for the buyer. Thus efficiency is really a measure of how effectively the production or service offerings of the business can support its customers.

Efficiency is one of the more difficult aspects of a business organization to assess from the outside. However, a number of measures can be used in most cases.

Productivity   Often productivity can be assessed through a number of the financial measures cited earlier. To these, we can add a quick evaluation by calculating the net revenue per employee. It is easily calculated by dividing the supplier's pretax profit (Earnings Before Taxes) by the number of employees in its company. Although not a sophisticated measurement, when evaluated in comparison to other potential suppliers, it can point out suppliers that operate more efficiently than their competitors, and vice-versa. This measure can be skewed, however, if the organization relies on outsourcing to any great extent since those employees would not be included in the count.

Two other measures commonly used to calculate productivity are Receivables Turnover Ratio and Inventory Turnover Ratio.

Receivables Turnover Ratio   The Receivables Turnover Ratio is a measure of how fast the organization is able to collect its outstanding accounts receivable, often a reflection of the liquidity of its customer base.

Receivables Turnover is calculated by dividing the current Accounts Receivable amount by the annual credit sales divided by 365. It can also be stated as 365 divided by the Receivables Turnover.

Inventory Turnover Ratio   The Inventory Turnover Ratio calculates how many times a business's inventory turns over—that is, is sold and replaced—during the year. Generally, a higher number indicates that inventory is moving quickly and being minimally stocked.

Inventory Turnover is calculated by dividing the cost of goods sold by the average value of inventory.

An Inventory Period Ratio can be calculated as 365 divided by Inventory Turnover.

MARKET SHARE   In simple terms, market share is the percentage of the total available market for a given product or service that the supplier has captured. It can be measured in terms of revenue (supplier's revenue divided by total market revenue) or, if a product, by units (supplier's unit sales divided by total market unit sales). Market share is a useful measure since it eliminates most of the effect of up-and-down economic conditions when considering the supplier's position in its market. A supplier with a small market share may be devoting its resources in other areas, thus providing very little support for that product or service; high market share may indicate sizable purchases by large companies and the potential for ignoring the needs of those with less purchasing power. Neither of these positions is universal, so checking is required.

CUSTOMERS AND REPUTATION   It's important to know who the supplier's customers are so that you can avoid any potential conflict of interest with one of your competitors, especially where proprietary information can be compromised. It is also important, as noted earlier, to know what share of the supplier's market your business will bring so that you can determine how well your voice will be heard.

Determining a supplier's reputation is important in understanding how well it services the market and how reliable its products or services are in the eyes of its customers and industry analysts. Here, for the most part, a measure of research will be needed to gain a clear picture of how the company is regarded.

Reference checks are another, very important way of determining a supplier's reputation. You should be prepared to interview several of the supplier's existing customers, asking for input regarding service reliability, quality, price escalation, and response to special needs. You can ask for reference contacts from the company or get a list of current customers and find the buyer yourself. It is important, though, to ask the exact same questions of each person you contact so that your "picture" of the supplier is as objective as you can make it.

If the supplier is controlled by any government regulatory agencies (such as the Environmental Protection Agency), it will be possible for you to check public records for a history of violations. A consistent record of violations, or violations that have not been resolved, should raise a red flag.

You also might consider whether the supplier has an effective procedure to monitor the satisfaction of its customers. Customer feedback helps in establishing a system and method by which the supplier will satisfy the needs of its customers. Without such processes in place, there is little assurance that the supplier has in fact fully responded to its customers' requirements. Determine the frequency of the surveys to establish the supplier's seriousness in conducting the process, what percentage of the customer base was included, and when the last survey was taken.

Comparative Evaluation Criteria: Operations

Operational measures focus on the specific activities of the supplier that can be easily learned of through public information or through a Request for Information. These measures include quality levels, order fulfillment metrics, capacity planning and scheduling accuracy, and risk management. Validation of the data is essential prior to selection, but unless the numbers appear unrealistic, the information provided by the suppliers can be used for competitive evaluation.

QUALITY MANAGEMENT PROCESS   There is a dual aspect to the characteristics of quality that most of us immediately recognize: First, quality means conformance to specifications. Conformance to specifications is another way of saying that we get exactly what we ordered. Second, quality means perceived value and desirability, such as an expensive, high-end automobile compared with a relatively low-priced, basic model.

Here we are concerned primarily with conformance to specifications; we discuss value in a later section. We employ quality control as a way of ensuring that we receive the product or service we specify and that we expect to a degree that is measureable. Thus we measure incoming product quality or the quality of services that have been performed. We must also consider how quality is controlled at the source by the provider in order to minimize the likelihood of receiving faulty products or services without the expense of performing incoming inspections.

Although typically quality is an operational concern, generally managed by the internal user group, supplier quality engineers are becoming increasingly common. Their role is to ensure the selection of quality-capable suppliers and to maintain metrics on failure rates so that corrective action, when needed, can take place as soon as possible.

In the next sections we touch on many of the elements of typical quality measures that sourcing teams should understand.

Certification   *Supplier certification* is one way of reducing (or eliminating altogether) the need for incoming inspection. In certifying a supplier, the buying organization typically determines that the supplier's internal system for measurement and control of quality is sufficient to ensure that it will meet the minimum quality level required without performing further incoming inspections. Often certification is provided on a part-by-part basis rather than as an overall blanket endorsement, so suppliers will need to "qualify" or recertify for each new part they produce.

When a supplier has been certified, it means that your organization will rely solely on the supplier's internal controls to produce acceptable quality. This process usually works fine, but there is one significant caveat: Since certification is based on the supplier's current processes (and equipment), your organization will need to know in advance when a supplier plans to change any production processes so that you can either recertify the process or reintroduce incoming inspection. The need for a proactive, compliant communication system to monitor these activities is evident, and you should carefully include this system as a requirement in your supplier certification agreement.

You should understand, also, that the Uniform Commercial Code requirement to inspect incoming materials in a reasonable period of time after receipt will still apply, and your organization will assume responsibility for the goods even if no incoming inspection is actually performed. In your agreement, you should extend liability for nonconforming parts to the supplier until the materials are actually used.

Acceptance Testing   Used most frequently when sourcing capital equipment, *acceptance testing* is a method used for determining if a particular piece of equipment is functioning at its expected output level prior to making final payment. It usually requires an engineering or manufacturing sign-off and a formal acknowledgment of acceptance (or rejection) communicated to the supplier.

The acceptance testing process is also commonly used for testing the first article submitted for approval prior to the supplier's actual manufacture runs and may represent a first step in the certification process.

Inspection Process   When used, the inspection process usually specifies a range of inspection frequency, extending from 100 percent inspection of all products to no inspection at all, or any level in between. In most cases, the buying organization may specify routine lot sampling on a random basis or at specific lots or time intervals, or it may require actual on-site audits of the process used by the supplier to measure quality.

The location of the inspection is important too. It is generally agreed that the earlier in the production process the inspection can take place, the less costly will be the corrective action. As a result, requirements may specify that the inspection will take place on the supplier's manufacturing line or at final assembly, or even as a separate process prior to shipment. Inspection may also be called for at your plant at various operational stages: at the receiving dock, upon release to manufacturing, or even at your final assembly stage.

Similarly, in a service environment, the results or output of the service can require inspection at a variety of times and places. Although it is not usual to perform acceptance testing as one might for equipment, there may be a requirement within the Statement of Work that calls for some method of services inspection at specified time intervals as part of gathering the metrics for a Service Level Agreement.

MEASURING QUALITY PERFORMANCE There's an adage that you "measure for success," since we have a known tendency to work toward specific goals. For this reason, the ongoing measurement of quality performance becomes critical to the success of any serious effort to generate improvements—keeping in mind, of course, that numerous methods for measurement are in common use today. Choosing the right measurement depends, to a large degree, on what we intend to accomplish.

Most of the time, the measurements we receive relating to quality performance will be based on some specific testing sequence. These measurements will tell us if the material or service conforms to our specifications or if the process being used to produce the products has the capability of doing the job.

We generally measure quality after the product or service has been received, or use a historical measurement of quality levels previously met, so ongoing measurement is not a function of sourcing. However, sourcing efforts must understand what *will* be measured so that a proper assessment of the supplier's ability to control quality can be made.

Some of the metrics commonly used in quality assessments include:

- **Statistical Process Control (SPC).** SPC is defined as a system that measures the actual distribution of events from the beginning to the end of a given process. It is a method of monitoring, controlling and, ideally, improving a process through statistical probability analysis. Its four basic steps include:

  1. Measuring the process
  2. Eliminating variances in the process to make it consistent

3. Monitoring the process
4. Improving the process to its best target value

When applied to quality measurement, SPC allows us to determine if the output of our process is within the desired range of control. Two key measures are used in SPC: the upper control limit—the highest point of measurement at which performance is acceptable—and the lower control limit—the lowest point of measurement at which performance is acceptable. Between these two points, events are considered acceptable and the process is considered to be in control.

We generally use SPC to measure the tolerances of products produced during rapidly repeating operational cycles, such as the output from automated machinery. In this environment, we determine the range of tolerance mathematically as 3 standard deviations above or below the average of the process.

> *Standard deviation* is a statistical measure of the variability or dispersion within a set of data points. It is calculated from the deviation or mathematical distance between each data value and the sample statistical mean and usually is represented by the Greek letter σ, "sigma." The more dispersed the data are, the larger the standard deviation. For data that follow a normal distribution, approximately 68 percent of all data will fall within 1 standard deviation of the sample mean, 95 percent of all values will fall within 2 standard deviations, and 99.7 percent of all data will fall within 3 standard deviations.

- **Six Sigma.** Six Sigma is a quality movement and improvement program that has grown from the process known as Total Quality Management. As a methodology, it focuses on controlling processes to $\pm$ 6 sigma (standard deviations) from a center line, which is the equivalent of 3.4 defects per million opportunities (where an opportunity is characterized as a chance of not meeting the required specification). Fundamental tenets of Six Sigma include reducing the variation within a process, improving system capability, and identifying essential factors that the customer views as crucial to quality.

  Six Sigma methodologies incorporate five steps corresponding to the acronym *DMAIC*:

  1. **D**efine customer requirement and improvement goals.
  2. **M**easure variables of the process.

3. **A**nalyze data to establish inputs and outputs.
4. **I**mprove system elements to achieve performance goals.
5. **C**ontrol the key variables to sustain the gains.

How a supplier employs Six Sigma methods to its operations is an important consideration in sourcing, since these methods have had a proven positive impact on the effectiveness of an organization's quality processes.

You can obtain further information about this process by visiting the American Society for Quality's web site at www.asq.org.

- **ISO Standards.** ISO, the International Organization for Standardization, was established in 1947 as an effort to consolidate widely dispersed methods of approaching quality standards. Its stated goal was to facilitate a means of coordinating, developing, and unifying industrial and technical quality standards. Based in Geneva, Switzerland, ISO is staffed by representatives from standards organizations in each of its member countries, working through committees that establish standards for industry, research, and government.

For sourcing, ISO compliance generally means assessing a series of quality assurance procedures that cover:
- An evaluation process for the selection of qualified vendors
- A periodic review of supplier performance, along with remedial action for unsatisfactory performance
- Documentation of quality requirements in the contract
- Quality control procedures for incoming material
- Establishment of quality systems and monitoring at suppliers' plants
- Procedures for tracking supplier defects and resolving quality issues with them
- Implementation of supplier training programs
- Collaboration in establishing joint quality assurance programs

ISO standards include:

- **ISO 9000.** In 1987, ISO issued a series of quality management and quality assurance standards as the ISO 9000 series. To date, these standards have been adopted by more than 500,000 organizations in 149 countries. This body of standards now provides a framework for customer-focused quality management throughout the global business community and has been widely acknowledged as providing the paradigm of assurance that customers will consistently find uniform quality in the products and services they purchase. Today organizations are certified as having achieved the standard through examination by an ISO registrar. Certified organizations may use certification as an assurance that standardized methods are being employed.

- **ISO 14000.** ISO 14000 is a series of international standards on environmental management. It provides a framework for the development of an environmental management and evaluation system and the supporting audit program. The standard does not prescribe environmental performance targets but instead provides organizations with the tools to assess and control the environmental impact of their activities, products, or services. The standards currently address Environmental Management Systems, environmental auditing, environmental labels and declarations, environmental performance evaluation, and life-cycle assessment.

  To learn more about this important set of standards, visit the ISO web site at www.iso.org.

- **Tolerances.** By definition, *tolerance* refers to the amount of deviation from our specification data points we are willing to accept. Tolerance is usually given in the same unit of measure or dimension as the specification.

  The associated concept of *tolerance stack-up* is used to measure the cumulative variations of each of the items in an assembly that goes into a final product. Tolerance stack-up analysis is used to determine if a form, fit, or function problem exists when manufacturing tolerances combine in a finished part or assembly. Tolerance stack-up analysis is typically performed by either assuming worst-case allowable dimensions or by using statistical analysis of tolerances.

- **Pareto charts.** The Pareto chart is a type of quality analysis used to determine if a few categories or units account for the majority of the total occurrences. The chart simply displays events in the order of their frequency.

  The commonly used Pareto principle (or 80/20 rule) was originally defined by J. M. Juran in 1950 and named after Vilfredo Pareto, a nineteenth-century Italian economist who studied the distribution of the world's wealth. Pareto concluded that the majority (80 percent) of the world's wealth was in the hands of a minority (20 percent) of its population.

  Figure 7.1 represents an example of a Pareto chart showing the percentage by category and the cumulative percentage of defects in a hypothetical failure analysis.

- **C_{pk}.** C_{pk} is a process capability *index*. Process capability analysis entails comparing the performance of a process against its specifications. A process is capable if virtually all of the possible variable values fall within the specification limits. It is measured numerically by using a capability index, C_p, with the formula:

$$C_p = \frac{\text{USL} - \text{LSL}}{6\sigma}$$

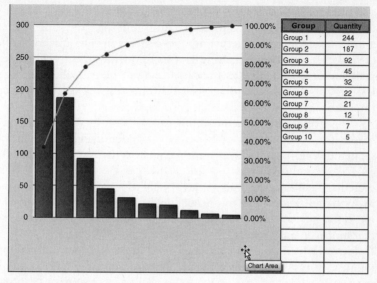

FIGURE 7.1 Pareto Chart

where

USL = upper specification limit
LSL = lower specification limit
σ = standard deviation

This equation indicates that the measure of process capability is how much of the observed process variation (USL − LSL) is covered by the process specifications. In this case, the process variation is measured by 6 standard deviations (±3 on each side of the mean). If C_p is greater than 1.0, then the process specification covers almost all of the process observations.

However, the C_p index does not account for a process that is off center. This equation can be modified to account for off-center processes to obtain the C_{pk} index as follows.

This equation takes the minimum distance between our specification limits and the process mean (stated as μ) and divides it by 3 standard deviations to arrive at the measure of process capability.

$$C_{pk} = \text{Minimum} \left[\text{USL} - \mu, \ \mu - \text{LSL} \right] / 3\sigma$$

■ **Benchmarking.** As it relates to quality considerations, *benchmarking* is the process of measuring your organization's performance against that of others within the same business sector or industry to determine what constitutes *best-in-class performance* and how it has been achieved. This comparison can form the basis for a quality improvement program targeting those areas where quality gaps or deviations exist. Benchmarking is also frequently used in conjunction with strategic value analysis and planning to help establish goals and allocate resources according to an overall organizational system of priorities.

Philosophically, benchmarking can be considered simply as the search for better methods. It is a way of identifying areas that need reengineering, change, and improvement. It is also a blend of both qualitative and quantitative research that can be tedious and painfully difficult to gather, consuming a great deal of resources. For this reason, many organizations turn to consultants and research organizations that are in the business of gathering this information as a way of accelerating the improvement process.

- **Defects.** Defects generally are measured in number per million opportunities, or parts per million (PPM) that are defective. This is a typical measure of the supplier's ability to control its operation.
- **Cost of poor quality.** The cost of poor quality is a difficult calculation to make on the fly since there are so many factors involved. Even with rough estimates, however, the numbers take on significance in terms of hard dollars. When poor quality results in the need for additional inspections or the return of a significant amount of sales, the cost escalates beyond what we anticipate. Under these conditions, the cost must be measured and reported and a plan for corrective action developed. It's easy to understand why a field replacement can cost far more than the original item, considering transportation costs, repair or replacement costs (you have essentially provided two for the price of one), and extra handling. The intangible costs of customer dissatisfaction also must be considered, even though they are not often possible to measure until sales begin to decline as a result.
- **Internal failure rates.** Internal failure rates are associated with built-in costs that are typically part of internal rework expenses that do not involve the customer. In most operations, these rates are calculated as a percentage of production expenses. When the measures increase beyond the normal statistical range, they are considered nonconforming to the acceptable standard.

EVALUATING ENGINEERING EXPERTISE   When evaluating a supplier's engineering expertise, we want to examine and assess the technology used in its product or service development to determine if it ensures delivering our requirements for quality and production capability. We also need to determine how well the organization develops and deploys up-to-date, competitive products or services that will have the longest possible life span in our market. Consider, too, how quickly the supplier can develop a new product to meet our specifications, relying on both engineering expertise and state-of-the-art equipment.

One way to evaluate engineering expertise is to compare the supplier's spending to that of other companies in its market for research and development, including testing and evaluation, as a percentage of its revenue. Of course, you must also determine how effective that spending is in producing results.

Engineering change management, and its accompanying documentation, is going to be a critical factor in evaluation as well. In industries that serve more advanced technology needs, a prototype commonly undergoes more than a dozen changes before production and several more in its early stages of marketing. Multiply this by the number of products or services the company produces, and you can see that without adequate processes for control, the change process could easily turn into a can of worms.

CONDUCTING SITE VISITS A site visit is one of the most powerful tools available to the sourcing team as a means of observing firsthand the supplier's operations and capabilities. It also provides the team with an opportunity to meet and evaluate key personnel who may have an impact on your business and with whom you will want continuing contact. Of course, not all acquisitions will require a site visit (it would be unusual for a team to visit its insurance underwriter, for example), so we direct our advice to those suppliers you believe are critical to your operations.

During the site visit, you and your team will be concerned primarily with determining the supplier's capabilities and, to the extent possible, its functional organization and operational systems. It is important that all sourcing team members collect as much documentation as possible, including their own observations, so that you don't have to rely on memory alone when comparing this supplier with its competitors should you need to conduct a site visit with more than one supplier.

The specific nature of the requirements being sourced will likely determine the characteristics that are important to observe during the visit, but there are some standard areas to consider:

- Does the supplier maintain a systematic, well-organized approach to operational planning? This is a priority requirement for you if on-time delivery is critical.

- How does the supplier monitor its production/service process to ensure a predictable level of quality?
  - Are its sampling and inspection methodologies effective?
  - Are its operational processes in line with sound management criteria?
  - Does it employ SPC and Six Sigma methodologies?
  - How are incoming inspections documented and tracked?
  - Is there a procedure in place for tracking field failures so that corrective action can be taken when appropriate?
  - Is there an approved quality manual?
  - Are internal and external audits conducted in appropriate intervals? (ISO or similar certification will provide evidence.)
- Are facilities well organized, with enough space for additional business?
- If applicable, are hazardous materials documented and controlled properly? Are separate areas set aside for their handling and storage?
- Can you assess the morale of the employees? Low morale generally results in costly high turnover and underskilled employees. You can also judge the work pace for an enthusiastic approach to the job and the interaction of employees as a way of evaluating the commitment to team work.
- Are standard operating procedures (SOPs) well documented and available to employees? Are employees knowledgeable about these procedures? If you have the opportunity to examine the SOPs, ask one or two questions about them to affected employees at random. Are they well informed?
- If equipment or testing and measuring devices are used, how are they calibrated, and is there evidence that the calibrations are current?
- Are the facilities or employees potentially susceptible to natural disasters (based on history), and, if so, are there contingency plans in place to ensure continuity?

This list is just a starting point, of course, and can be expanded to whatever degree is required to ensure the supplier's operations will serve your needs. What is important, though, is that you and the sourcing team are well prepared in advance with a set of questions and a list of areas to examine, documented so that you can ensure that the same criteria are used for other suppliers being considered for the project.

SUPPLIER SELECTION   With a clearly documented set of evaluation criteria that you intend to use to assess and select the supplier on hand, you will be ready to select the best supplier. In this regard, we are going to propose two best practice concepts: value-based source selection and the scorecard for competitive evaluation.

Value-Based Supplier Selection

We want to use best value as the overriding consideration in situations where price is not the single controlling factor (as in off-the-shelf products or standardized services). To do so effectively requires a consistent and clearly defined approach, so let's explore what we mean by best value and how it can be evaluated.

BEST VALUE DEFINED   "Best value," according to the U.S. Federal Acquisition Regulations, "means the expected outcome of an acquisition that, in the Government's estimation, provides the greatest overall benefit in response to the requirement." Another federal agency, the Federal Highway Administration, which is managed by the Department of Transportation, describes it this way:

> *The overall maximum value of the proposal to a sponsor after considering all of the evaluation factors described in the specifications for the project including but not limited to the time needed for performance of the contract, innovative design approaches, the scope and quality of the work, work management, aesthetics, project control, and total project cost of the formulas or other criteria for establishing the parameters for the Best Value are generally clearly defined with the goal of being objective.*

Although it sounds simple—"who offers the best deal"—the process of evaluation can be challenging and difficult to duplicate from one acquisition to another since the criteria can be so different.

Typically, assessing the best value in supplier selection relies on the method of selecting the best of several alternatives that are available. In effect, doing this amounts to performing a trade-off analysis since rarely do all suppliers propose the same combination of factors so that you can simply pick the one with the highest offer. In fact, in many cases, there are no tangible metrics on which to even base an evaluation.

BEST VALUE FACTORS   Price and associated costs always play a dominant role in source selection; however, a best value approach also takes into account nonprice factors that offer the greatest benefit in terms of performance, risk management, and other intangible factors.

These factors represent the key areas of importance and emphasis to be considered in the source selection decision. However, they must support a meaningful comparison and discrimination between and among competing proposals. Thus the evaluation examines all factors comparatively in an attempt to quantify the relative importance of key factors such as:

- **Price.** "Price" refers to the overall cost of acquiring the product or service. Often we consider "landed price," which includes the cost of the goods plus transportation and duties (where they apply). In sourcing equipment, we might also consider the concept of Total Cost of Ownership, a method for evaluating the lowest cost of equipment after accounting for each element of associated cost during its lifetime: installation, maintenance, replacement parts, employee training, and disposal.
- **Quality.** Quality can be calculated as the cost of poor quality—for example, field replacement, scrap, inspection, and related elements (as covered in the previous section). We also evaluate the expected level of defects, comparing it to industry standards and competitors.
- **Technical capability.** Technical capability includes unique designs or advanced technology that increases sales. It might cover how the supplier employs technology, either internally or with its customers. It could also evaluate how the supplier is positioned in the marketplace as a developer of new technology.
- **Lead time.** Time is always a valuable commodity; time to market for new product or service offerings of your business assumes a key role in best value analysis. Often this measure assesses how well the supplier meets its deadlines based on input from existing customers or its own records.
- **Service.** Service consists of a combination of factors that includes technical support, warranty coverage, and replacements. Service also relates to how well the supplier satisfies its existing customers and how well it carries out its responsibilities. Service might also measure how well the supplier responds to customer complaints or requests for information.
- **Process improvement.** Process improvement rates the supplier's internal systems for driving continuous improvement, driving added value in all categories over time.

These are, of course, the obvious characteristics we examine. Overall, however, we want to take into account any factors that justify acceptance of other than the lowest bid.

Scorecard

The evaluation scorecard is a useful method for summarizing the input of team members and comparing the evaluation of suppliers to one another. Prior to beginning the evaluation, team members and advisors must be familiar with the following items for the current project:

- Request for Proposal (what is being procured)
- Acquisition plan

- Methodology/best practices
- Evaluation process
- Evaluation criteria and standards

To enable an objective evaluation, it is important to rely primarily on measurable factors. Here is a hypothetical example of a measurable evaluation factor, an element of the technical criteria. It defines the requirement, explains what is being evaluated, and states a standard for measuring the response:

Requirement

Provide rapid on-site network printer repair to ensure a maximum downtime of 30 minutes.

Criterion

This factor evaluates the adequacy of the proposed technical approach for quick, on-site recovery from network printer failure.

Standard

Proposed technical approach provides credible means to reliably recover from all network printer failures within 30 minutes.

Using a scale of 1 to 4, you can establish a specific set of evaluation criteria. Note the progressively increasing value going up the scale:

Meets the Standard = 1

Proposal A: Printer will be equipped with a standard spare parts pack including removal and replacement tools.

Slightly Above Standards = 2

Proposal B: Printer will be equipped with a standard spare parts pack including removal and replacement tools along with a 24/7 800 number for service support.

Significantly Above Standards = 3

Proposal C: Spare printers will be available for customer installation in all buildings.

Exceeds Standards and Expectations = 4

Proposal D: Spare printers will be available in all buildings and will automatically replace any out-of-service printer through network rerouting.

Once you have determined which criteria you wish to rate, you can develop a rating matrix. Table 7.1 shows one example.

TABLE 7.1 Simple Scorecard Layout

	Overall Weight	Question A	Question B	Question C	Total Score
Price					
Quality					
Service					
Technology					
	= 1.00				

Notice that each major category, such as Price or Quality, is broken down into further subelements or criteria referred to here as Questions. For example, under Price, you might want to consider how this price compares to other offers, how frequently the supplier increases its price, or what the supplier's discount structure for larger volumes of service is.

Or in the example of the network printers, this would become a Service question: How will you support a maximum downtime of 30 minutes for each printer?

The overall weighting must equal 1 or 100, so each category would be a fraction of that. Thus, each question would be given a score based on the individual rating factor and would be multiplied by the overall category weight.

As a first step, establish the category criteria and their weights. Table 7.2 shows how the categories might be divided. Often this division is based on the organization's current needs—emphasizing Price, for example, over all other categories.

TABLE 7.2 Adding Overall Weighting

	Overall Weight	Question A	Question B	Question C	Total Score
Price	.35				
Quality	.30				
Service	.20				
Technology	.15				
	=1.00				

In the second step, develop the evaluation questions for each of the categories. Table 7.3 shows the examples for price questions according to the guidelines noted earlier.

TABLE 7.3 Evaluation Subsets (Questions)

	Overall Weight	Question A	Question B	Question C	Total Score
Price	.35	Comparative amount	Length of stability	?	
Quality	.30				
Service	.20				
Technology	.15				
	= 1.00				

In the third step, determine the scaling to be used (see Table 7.4). Rate the input to the question on a sliding scale of perhaps 1 to 5 or 1 to 4 (if you want to avoid any fence sitting).

TABLE 7.4 Scaling

	Overall Weight	Question A	Question B	Question C	Total Score
Price	.35	1–5?	0–6?		
Quality	.30				
Service	.20				
Technology	.15				
	= 1.00				

In a simple example, you might score the supplier's response as shown in Table 7.5.

TABLE 7.5 Scoring

	Overall Weight	Question A	Question B	Question C	Total Score
Price	.35	2	2	4	
Quality	.30	3	3	3	
Service	.20				
Technology	.15				
	= 1.00				

In the fourth step, calculate the total weighted score (see Table 7.6). This is simply the sum of the score earned in that category multiplied by the weighting factor. Here the total in the price category is 8, which is multiplied by the weighting factor .35 to produce a weighted score of 2.8: $(8 \times .35 = 2.8)$.

TABLE 7.6 Calculation

	Overall Weight	Question A	Question B	Question C	Total Score
Price	.35	2	2	4	8
Quality	.30	3	3	3	
Service	.20				
Technology	.15				
	= 1.00				

Finally, if we line up the averages for three suppliers, we can get a clearer picture of how the comparison might work. In Table 7.7, we can see that Supplier C is the clear choice, scoring higher than competitors in each of the categories. If there were any category that might not be conclusive, it is technology, where the range of scoring is relatively tight.

TABLE 7.7 Summing Up

	Overall Weight	Supplier A	Supplier B	Supplier C
Price	.35	2.80	1.90	3.25
Quality	.30	2.70	2.00	2.80
Service	.20	1.60	1.60	2.20
Technology	.15	1.65	1.55	1.80
Total		> 8.75	> 7.05	> 10.05

Please keep in mind that this is a relatively simple example. With a little effort, you should be able to find much more detailed examples on the Internet. A more thorough example can be found in the white paper "Supplier Evaluation Framework Based on Balanced Scorecard with Integrated Corporate Social Responsibility Perspective" by Worapon Thanaraksakul and Busaba Phruksaphanrat, available at: www.iaeng.org/publication/ IMECS2009/IMECS2009_pp1929-1934.pdf.

Summary

This chapter examined the various evaluation criteria and how they relate to the sourcing and selection of a supplier. Evaluation criteria can be segmented into those elements that focus on business and those that focus on operations.

The business criteria most commonly used include historical data, financial analysis (measures of liquidity, profitability, and efficiency), market share, customers, and reputation. Operations criteria include quality management processes and measurement systems, evaluating engineering expertise, and conducting site visits.

We concluded the chapter with a description of supplier selection linked to best value criteria and provided a simple method for using a scorecard to help determine which supplier offers the greatest benefits.

CHAPTER 8

Negotiation Revisited

Clearly, there are many areas of real and potential differences in the buying versus the selling business positions. There are matters of defining and interpreting specifications, rationalizing quantity and delivery requirements with production or capacity constraints, and, surely, notions of what constitutes fair and reasonable supplier pricing. These differences cannot always be resolved by the competitive process alone, so negotiation must be employed to complement that process.

To rephrase this somewhat: Negotiation is employed whenever there are differences of objectives, interests, or points of view that must be resolved in order for two or more parties to reach agreement.

Negotiation is a *process* of reaching agreement through discussion, analysis, and bargaining. It is not an event. It is not a game. It is not a sport. It is a process. It has an easily identified methodology, with clearly defined planning steps that, when followed, produce the final results we want...or get us as close to the results as we can possibly come.

The Nature of Negotiation

Negotiation is both collaborative and competitive. What demands skill in negotiation is the ability to deal effectively with the duality in the process itself. On one hand, there is the intrinsic intent to reach an agreement. That makes the process cooperative. After all, isn't that the very reason why we enter into negotiation in the first place? On the other hand, there are those areas of real and perceived differences. And resolving them to one or the other's advantage makes the process competitive.

The competitive nature of negotiation is the prime reason why some of us are intimidated by it. After all, in any competitive endeavor or contest, there are winners and losers, and if we negotiate, we could wind up on the losing side. This concern is not typically consciously thought out. Rather, it's more subliminal or subconscious. The result is that we rationalize why we can't or shouldn't negotiate: "We don't have the time," "What's the point? We already have competitive quotations." The risk of losing is intimidating and often results in avoidance of the negotiation process altogether.

According to Lou DeRose of DeRose Associates:

We can never develop and apply negotiating skills unless we overcome the negative attitudes we may have about the process. And this begins when we realize the need to negotiate, and the self-interest we have in satisfying that need. I have seen all kinds of money and time expended on "negotiation training." All too often, these efforts jump immediately to the "how-to" of negotiating, with little or no attention paid to the rationale, the whys, of negotiating. It has been my experience that if this rationale is not provided, those who are "trained" to negotiate will not do so. They may find the training exercises stimulating, even fun. But they will not employ what they have "learned." Learning means that the learner changes his or her way of doing things, and if one's attitude towards negotiation remains negative, they've truly not learned to negotiate.

We would like to show you how this fear can be overcome and how you can go about "bargaining" with the same professionalism you demonstrate in your other sourcing activities. We can accomplish this by removing the veil of mystery surrounding the negotiation process.

Negotiation Strategy

Successful negotiation demands a carefully developed planning strategy that addresses the dual aspects of negotiation: collaboration and competition. The cooperative, collaborative aspects are addressed by focusing on issues that can be easily agreed on. The competitive aspect addresses issues that are in disagreement; issues that are unclear, ambiguous, in dispute, or subject to different interpretation or opinion. Before you begin any serious negotiation, you must identify and characterize which issues are priorities so that you can appropriately focus your planning energies on them.

An effective negotiation planning strategy must take into account your objectives and those of your supplier, identifying issues that favorably and unfavorably impact each of them. Along these lines, negotiation planning strategy generally needs to address long-term mutual satisfaction and the development of an approach that seeks to maximize the benefits to both parties, so that each party can leave the negotiating table feeling successful. Without a clearly defined set of negotiation plan goals, there is no way of knowing what you have achieved, and both parties will continue to look back with regret.

Broad Outcomes

Negotiation is not always a game or a sport. In games and sports there is rarely more at stake than the outcome: only a winner and loser. In negotiation, there are situations where both parties win and situations where both parties lose, in effect creating three options counting the win/lose. As part of developing your negotiation plan, it is important to determine which of the outcomes you would be willing to accept. Making a determination will certainly affect your objectives, your concessions, and your acceptable offers in each of the elements you are bargaining for. Later on, during the actual negotiation, this previously determined outcome will drive your negotiation tactics.

Why Negotiate

One of the serious problems in relying solely on the competitive bidding process for source selection and pricing is that relevant issues that should be addressed up front are not addressed at all. Too often this results in one or the other party being dissatisfied when these issues materialize or rise to the surface. We negotiate to address those issues, identify areas that are ambiguous or in dispute, and then resolve them. Doing so results in an agreement that better ensures achieving the negotiation objectives we seek, but at the same time is mutually satisfying.

When to Negotiate

An essential aspect of negotiation is determining when to negotiate. How can competition alone resolve important issues concerning unique design or application requirements? Competition has severe limitations in ensuring value when requirements are special only to you, or when they are complex and technically demanding.

Suppose the Statement of Work calls for performance above and beyond existing technology or state of the art. You need to ensure that the right engineering and fulfillment processes will be employed to get the job done properly. Would you be comfortable depending on competitive bidding alone to resolve those issues for you? Unlikely. Competition is never going to be fully effective when the risks involved in the purchase are significant.

In situations such as these, negotiation is the clear choice as the path to fully achieving our key negotiation planning objectives. Without the additional effort invested in negotiation, the competitive bidding process *alone* will likely come up short of achieving our objectives. The bidding process may produce the best offer, but it is only through the negotiation process that we can fully maximize our bargain.

There are also situations when an opportunity exists for improving an initial proposal based on information we have received from other bidders—perhaps pricing can be reduced or payment terms extended. In situations of potentially high risk, we may want to negotiate for stronger contingency planning efforts. Where technical requirements are complex, we may want to see some additional engineering effort factored in. When bidding competition is limited, suppliers have little incentive to provide full value, and we may be compelled to negotiate in order to achieve it.

What to Negotiate

It's a common but astute adage that *everything is negotiable*. Your job, then, is to prioritize what you want to negotiate given the specific circumstances of the acquisition. Consider all of these common elements first and then go on to others that may present themselves during the course of negotiation activities:

- Price
- Payment terms
- Deliverables
- Service levels
- Quality
- Support
- Warranties
- Risk assumption
- Business continuity/disaster recovery
- Liquidated damages
- Insurance/bonding
- Freight allowances (for product)
- Consignment inventory

Concessions by your supplier in any of these or similar elements will always increase the value of the acquisition.

Value

In negotiations, value can be described as the total perceived worth, importance, or usefulness of the items bargained for, often measured in terms of what we agree to exchange for them.

Negotiation Planning

It is often noted that the outcome of any negotiation is proportionate to the degree of planning or homework that goes into it. If you expect to achieve the full potential of an agreement, to maximize the benefits of the negotiated agreement, recognize that you must develop a detailed plan that you and your team will follow. The three most important elements in negotiation are planning, planning, and planning (to paraphrase a well-worn cliché). Our recommended strategy, therefore, is to achieve our *objectives* through careful and thorough planning.

A negotiation plan is used to develop a comprehensive course of action. Actions are linked to a well-defined set of objectives. The plan outlines the likely points of agreement and disagreement with the supplier. The plan also addresses the resources that must be employed to achieve these objectives in terms of time, people, and required information. And, as we discuss shortly, to be effective, a negotiation plan requires that we understand the supplier's objectives as fully as possible so that we can establish a set of concessions that we can offer in exchange for the supplier's concessions.

Although there is that competitive aspect to negotiation, the basic purpose of the process is to reach mutual agreement. That's implicit in the very act of sitting down to talk. Why consent to a meeting if reaching an agreement were not the earnest intent of the parties? This is what makes the process, to some degree, cooperative. Tailor your strategy, then, around what's positive. Identify areas on which you can easily agree. The more of these you can identify, and relate to other issues, the more you broaden the base for a mutually satisfactory agreement and build supplier relationships and understandings. At its best, negotiation planning prepares the way for future tactical operations and establishes a pattern of collaboration essential to achieving negotiation objectives.

Before getting into the details of how to develop a negotiation plan, we should understand that there are three phases in the negotiation process: analysis, discussion, and bargaining. Briefly, let's look at what these terms mean:

1. **Analysis.** The analysis process is a method used to evaluate the supplier's strengths and weaknesses and how the supplier is likely to respond to your requests. It can include the supplier's past history, market conditions, and potential motivating factors attributable to its current business situation. Your analysis will help you discover gaps in the information you need for planning and what areas you may need to investigate further.
2. **Discussion.** Effective discussion aims to build an amicable and cooperative climate so that agreement can be reached more easily. It is

positive, stressing the favorable and constructive aspects of your and the other party's relationship. Effective discussion is always an exercise in skillful communication and motivation.

Discussion is also a means to discover the major needs and objectives of the supplier with whom you will be negotiating, in an informal atmosphere where questions are asked and answered in a learning mode. It will also be helpful in filling the gaps discovered during your initial analysis.

3. **Bargaining.** *Quid pro quo* is a Latin term that means, literally, "this for that." In the realm of negotiation, this term is used to describe a *bargain* as "something for something." Bargaining is the medium for exchange in the negotiation process: The more we get of what we want, and the less we concede to get it, the greater is our objective benefit; the less we get and the more we give up, the less is our objective benefit.

Developing a Negotiation Plan

The process of developing a negotiation plan requires identifying a logical, sequential set of steps. This may be an extensive undertaking requiring a great deal of research and team interaction, or it may entail just a few minutes to jot down a simple approach. The amount of time and work you put into your plan will, of course, depend on the nature of the sourcing project.

Sourcing for a customized piece of equipment or a complex service necessitates extensive research and planning. Similarly, considerable effort is required to develop a long-term supplier partnership for products or services that are critical to achieving your organization's strategic objectives. If you add to the mix a product or service that uses very recently developed technology, you may spend weeks or even months in the planning process. If, however, you are sourcing for an urgent, unplanned need, your time will be extremely limited and will significantly reduce (or eliminate) the amount of time available for planning.

All of these demands and limitations can add a great deal of complexity to a sourcing project so it becomes even more important to understand and master the negotiation planning process. Next we outline the main elements of this process in a relatively simple manner so that we don't obscure the basics.

Selecting a Team

It is important to plan and conduct negotiation with a cross-functional team since negotiation can become quite complex, both administratively and technically, and can be impossible for one individual to manage. Procurement makes the award and should lead the negotiation team. Other team members would include representatives from Operations and the user group, along with other key stakeholders, such as finance, environmental health and safety, legal, quality assurance, information technology, logistics, and facilities, depending on the nature of what it is that's being negotiated.

Team members need not be present during the actual negotiations. In fact, there are times when it is undesirable to have them present; however, they can and should act as advisors prior to the actual negotiation and can be used to review the agreement prior to signature as a sanity check.

When team members do attend the actual negotiation sessions, they should be thoroughly familiar with the adopted negotiation plan and carefully coached on their specific roles during the tactical procedure. It is always best to have only one spokesperson, so rules should be established to break for a team caucus whenever questions or conflicts arise rather than having the issues presented to the supplier before a firm position can be established. There will be times, of course, when you will have to ask a team member if the proposal you are about to accept meets the organization's needs, but be sure to make it clear to the team, in advance, that great care needs to be taken in responding so that no commitment is made prematurely.

Developing Objectives

You can develop objectives for negotiation in a number of ways. One way is by comparing the Request for Proposal (RFP) response of the supplier with whom you intend to negotiate to other proposals you have received for the same RFP. Doing so will enable you to find gaps in this supplier's proposal that may be open to negotiations. As a simple example, let's say you intend to negotiate with Supplier A for a printer maintenance program since overall its offer provides the best value. However, Supplier B offers a viable proposal that contains a maximum downtime of 12 hours whereas Supplier A's proposal is for 24 hours. Considering that both suppliers are equally responsive, you have identified a gap in maximum downtime of 12 hours that is subject to further negotiation.

Another common way to develop objectives is to compare the user's requirements to the proposal, point by point. Wherever you can identify a gap between the requirements and the supplier's offer, you have a point for negotiation.

Analyzing the supplier's proposal in light of market conditions provides another way to identify areas for negotiation; if the market exhibits declining utilization of capacity, you may expect prices to fall in the near term. You will then offer an additional justification for negotiating lower prices.

Objectives should be formulated with the SMART concept in mind, meaning that objectives are *s*pecific, *m*easurable, *a*ttainable, *r*elevant, and *t*ime-bound. It helps very little to enter a negotiation with the objective of "gaining a price reduction." To be specific and measurable, a price reduction objective needs to be stated in terms of an amount, either in dollars or in a percentage. To be attainable, a price reduction objective needs to be in alignment with current market trends and the supplier's ability to sustain operations at that pricing. In terms of relevancy, a price reduction objective must apply to the current acquisition and fall within the scope of your negotiation. To be time-bound, a price reduction objective needs to refer to the specific period that it covers. You can apply this concept to virtually all of your negotiation objectives.

For each objective, it is important to select a minimum and maximum range within which your team can support an agreement. Let's say your market research indicates excess capacity in the industry so you believe a 10 percent reduction from the original proposal is in line with current conditions. Recognizing the give-and-take nature of the bargaining process, you would want to open discussions at a somewhat higher (but realistic) number to create a potential concession if needed by reducing that demand somewhat, so perhaps you might start at 14 percent. You would also want to recognize a point at which you will never be able to accept an offer—your walk-away position; perhaps 7 percent. No agreement can be reached unless the offering price is reduced by 7 percent.

This, of course, is a hypothetical example. In fact, it would actually be advantageous not to open the bargaining with any number, even a large one, until you know what range the supplier is willing to offer. What if the supplier has padded its quote based on market conditions that no longer exist and subsequently recognizes that the offer made can no longer be justified? What if there is an opening offer to reduce pricing by 20 percent in exchange for an immediate contract?

As you determine these numbers or conditions for your objectives, record them in a document such as the matrix in Table 8.1.

Also, keep in mind that you may be asked to justify your requirement just as you might want the supplier to justify its position. You should be prepared, in a collaborative manner, to explain just why you feel your demand is justified and what is driving it from your organization's perspective. The supplier should not ask for this information in a challenging way; nor should it be taken as a challenge. It should be presented as a fact-finding process to better understand opposing positions. A series of well-constructed "why" questions could generate information that will frame your negotiation position.

TABLE 8.1 Negotiation Objectives Matrix

Objectives	Opening	Target	Walk-Away	Concession(s)
Price reduction	14%	10%	7%	A. Offer an immediate contract B. Offer an option to extend contract for an additional year
Completion/ delivery	4 weeks	6 weeks	8 weeks	Reduction in element x of the quality requirements
Extend to all objectives				

Prioritizing Objectives to Match Concessions

In most situations, you will have a limited number of concessions available. These are like poker chips: Once they are gone, you will have to fold your cards and move on. Therefore, it's extremely important to ration your concessions so that you don't use them up before you have achieved those objectives that are critical to you and your team. You can do this by clearly linking each concession to a specific objective. Doing so will enable you to plan out your concessions realistically. If you don't organize your plan in this way, you will be in danger of using your concessions disproportionately in exchange for weaker concessions by the supplier. You are also in danger of using your concessions before achieving most of your objectives. How you use concessions, in a way, is the heart of your negotiation plan.

Supplier's Objectives

Another requirement for negotiation planning is to attempt to recognize the supplier's objectives in order to better understand what you may be able to gain through an exchange of concessions. If, for example, you are aware that the supplier is operating well below capacity, you might be able to gain a price reduction by committing to more volume in the earlier stages of the contract.

In many cases, you can determine what the supplier hopes to achieve during initial discussions and through analysis. There are times when a supplier will be completely up front in describing its objectives so there will generally be less speculation. However, you always want to be prepared in the event that the supplier raises additional requirements during the negotiation or drops those previously stated. Sometimes, in fact, misstating objectives is actually a planned tactic used to generate a bit of confusion in order to obtain greater concessions from the buyer.

SWOT Analysis

Some negotiation planners like to begin their approach with a SWOT (strengths, weaknesses, opportunities, and threats) analysis, as described in Chapter 1. You would typically conduct this analysis just after establishing objectives.

As you conduct the analysis, you might discover that your strengths rely on the competitive landscape, for example, that allows you a number of choices in suppliers. The supplier's weaknesses might be the need to obtain a contract right away to avoid a layoff. Market conditions that see prices rising may turn out to be a threat to your ability to negotiate reductions; conversely, falling prices may be a threat to the supplier, compelling concessions in exchange for an immediate contract.

It's common to find that a particular strength of one party is a weakness for the other. Similarly, a threat to one may turn out to be an opportunity for the other. However, these conditions need to be monitored since there may not be a one-to-one relationship.

Agenda/Order of Discussion

One of the most powerful tools, often overlooked, can be control of the agenda. If you can control the order of bargaining during a negotiation, you will have a much better chance of staying on track with your negotiation plan concessions.

One way to accomplish this control is to prepare an initial draft of an agenda that follows your order of precedence prior to the actual negotiation. Once this is submitted to the supplier for adoption, and approved, you will be able to refer back to it during negotiation. Doing so will go a long way in helping to maintain your focus on tying concessions to negotiation objectives.

Staying Organized

During a negotiation, it is critical that you and your team stay fully organized, for obvious reasons. Everyone on your team attending the negotiation needs to be clear on the order of discussion and the agreed-on objectives. One way to do so is by using a matrix, such as the one shown earlier in Table 8.1. That table presents a very simple example with only objectives; yours will likely contain a great deal more detail. You can also add a column on the right to record your agreed-on terms.

Tactics

Negotiation is not always a game or a sport. In sports, there is rarely more than one outcome: a winner and a loser. In negotiation, there are situations where both parties win and situations where both parties lose, creating, in effect, three options counting the win/lose. As part of developing your negotiation plan, it is important to determine which of the outcomes you would be willing to accept.

We are not going to discuss tactics in this book. The use of tactics by a negotiator is both personal to an individual's style and specific to the circumstances, so there are endless permutations for every particular element, similar in complexity to a chess game. It would not do justice to the topic if we attempt to discuss it here or even in its own chapter. You will be better served by selecting a source that deals with negotiation tactics in depth.

Exception Conditions

There are always going to be exceptions to a standard format for planning negotiations. Some situations, which we briefly discuss here, can be readily anticipated.

Negotiating in a Single-/Sole-Source Situation

Conducting negotiations with a single- or sole-source supplier presents some challenges. In many ways, you may lose the leverage you would normally have in a competitive situation. That's why your negotiation plan should take this into account.

Primarily, you will need to be prepared to more fully justify your demands in this situation and to link them to very specific concessions that you know the supplier will want to accept. Be prepared to come to the table with well-documented facts. For example, provide third-party analysis for deteriorating sales in the particular market segment or provide articles that establish that there is a consensus of industry analysts that the pricing trends are pointed downward. Similarly, you must establish the value of concessions in some objective manner, typically through demonstrated cost savings to the supplier. Show how your concessions will offset the cost of the concessions you are asking for.

Cross-Cultural Negotiation

While this is the final section of the chapter, it is by no means the least important. It is simply the most logical position for the topic.

It is easy to understand that culture plays a huge role in negotiating with companies located in another country. As we develop our negotiation plan, we need to make adjustments according to the nature of the business and social culture in which the supplier is located. Although these adjustments mainly impact our tactical approach, there are some strategic elements that will need to be addressed.

Probably the most pronounced differences between cultures lie in the role of the individual, how each individual views issues, and how each communicates in a business environment. In a cross-cultural negotiation, these are important considerations that may determine its outcome.

What is most important universally is that we prepare our negotiation plan to reflect the in-depth research we have conducted. This will help us to better understand the critical factors in the culture in which we are going to operate. Obviously, this is an enormous topic, the subject of many books, so we will attempt to go no further than to note the areas that are important to take into account. Please consider them as you read through this section; think about how you might develop an analysis of conditions and how you might be inclined to deal with them. Consider also how you and your team operate and how you appear to those from another culture in terms of the next points.

- **Strategy.** The choice of a strategy is going to be affected by cultural orientation. Some cultures avoid confrontation at all costs and much prefer a less aggressive approach. This will, in turn, lead to a more collaborative environment. At the other end of the continuum, you might find so-called power negotiators who do not oppose using confrontational tactics if doing so leads to striking a better bargain for themselves.
- **Leadership.** Culture will likely determine who will be the lead negotiator. In some cultures, leadership is in the hands of senior management; in others, it may be conducted by junior members but will require approval according to the chain of command. Some cultures will not allow women to play a leading role (or any role at all) within the negotiation process.
- **Team size.** Countries where teams are consensus driven rather than individualistic are likely to favor larger teams. Team size is likely to impact the amount of time it will take to reach agreement.
- **Conducting negotiations.** The process and style of conducting negotiations is also largely driven by culture. It includes the amount of information the supplier is willing to divulge as well as the amount of engaged communication likely to take place. Culture may also determine how tough the supplier's team might be in granting concessions.
- **Communication.** How much communication takes place will also be closely linked to a culture. Team-oriented, consensus-driven cultures will rely heavily on communications whereas individualistic cultures may value very little communication.

Communication can also be described in some very simple terms.

Communication

Methods of communication vary among cultures. Some emphasize direct and simple methods of communication; others rely heavily on indirect and complex methods. The latter may use circumlocutions, figurative forms of speech, facial expressions, gestures and other kinds of body language. In a culture that values directness, such as the American or the Israeli, you can expect to receive a clear and definite response to your proposals and questions. In cultures that rely on indirect communication, such as the Japanese, reaction to your proposals may be gained by interpreting seemingly vague comments, gestures, and other signs. What you will not receive at a first meeting is a definite commitment or rejection.

Source: Jeswald W. Salacuse, "The Top Ten Ways that Culture Can Affect Your Business Negotiation," *Ivey Business Journal* online (March/April 2004).

Communication often takes place nonverbally. Thus, one must become aware of how nonverbal communication operates within the given culture and, frequently, within many of its subcultures. This can be learned, of course, and it will be quite beneficial to take the time to learn the meanings of common body language and other signals.

We in the West tend to avoid ambiguity; we like everything to be clear in black and white. This is certainly not the case in many other parts of the world, where ambiguity is much more an acceptable condition. Although Westerners generally need to conclude with an agreement, people from some other cultures are not uncomfortable letting the issues pass to be dealt with at a later time.

- **Relationships.** Many cultures are relationship driven. Individuals need the opportunity to get to know one another, and socializing is one way of doing so. In this situation, attempting to rush the process will be counterproductive; doing so will simply confuse and upset those you are going to negotiate with. In effect, socializing is not really social; it is an integral part of conducting business.

Salacuse also reminds us of this important consideration: "As a general rule, it is always safer to adopt a formal posture and move to an informal stance, if the situation warrants it, than to assume an informal style too quickly."

In addition, as Salacuse quotes from *Cross-Cultural Negotiations* by Paul R. Horst, Jr.:

[W]hen doing business internationally, we need to consider:

1. *The negotiating environment*
2. *Cultural and sub-cultural differences*
3. *Ideological differences*
4. *Foreign bureaucracy*
5. *Foreign laws and governments*
6. *Financial insecurity due to international monetary factors*
7. *Political instability and economic changes*

Summary

In this chapter, we examined the importance of a negotiation plan and its key elements. We provided an overview of the nature of negotiation itself and the negotiation strategy. This included sections on broad outcomes, why we negotiate, when to negotiate, and what to negotiate.

The section covering negotiation planning examined the requirements for analysis, discussion, and bargaining. In more detail, we covered team selection, developing objectives, and prioritizing objectives to match concessions. We also discussed taking into account the supplier's objectives, the position of SWOT analysis, and creating an agenda or order of discussion. This was followed with a planning matrix to help keep the process well organized. We concluded with the requirements for negotiating in a single- or sole-source situation.

CHAPTER 9

Supplier Diversity

The concept of supplier diversity programs to support economically disadvantaged groups in the United States was born from the American sense of fairness and equality, and supported by numerous government-sponsored programs that have been legislated into law. But many of us are not familiar with the nature and benefits of a diversity supplier program, and, importantly, many do not fully understand how their organization can support and benefit from these programs.

As it relates to sourcing management, supplier diversity programs expand the organization's supply base by developing new sources of sustainable supply as a means to expand competition. Diversity programs support a supply base that is generally more representative of the community than it would be without such programs, since diversity sources are generally local businesses. We call this process "inclusion." Fostering inclusion supports the economic welfare of the community and promotes the availability of a viable workforce. Thus by increasing the diversity of the supply base, we also increase its overall economic health. That is why we chose to include the process in our examination of best practices in sourcing management.

Diversity Programs

When we speak of "diversity," we refer primarily to historically underrepresented segments of our society; initially these were small businesses owned by minorities. Government has expanded the definition to include other segments of small business that require special consideration: service-disabled veteran-owned small business, disabled veteran-owned small business, veteran-owned small business, and women-owned small business. Also included are small businesses located in specific historically underutilized business zones called HUBZones. As a group, all these businesses are referred to using the acronym MWDBEs (minority, women, and disadvantaged business enterprises) or sometimes just SDBs (small, disadvantaged businesses) and MBEs (minority business enterprises).

Definitions and Certification

Two major entities define what type of business is part of a disadvantaged business group: the U.S. Small Business Administration (SBA) and the National Minority Supplier Development Council (NMSDC).

THE U.S. SMALL BUSINESS ADMINISTRATION   The SBA administers two particular business assistance programs for SDBs: the 8(a) Business Development Program and the Small Disadvantaged Business Certification Program. Until recently, the SBA certified small businesses that were "disadvantaged." Currently, this process has been suspended, and organizations seeking to do business with the federal government as small, disadvantaged businesses can self-certify for any of the protected categories. The 8(a) Program, however, is still in effect.

The 8(a) Program—named for Section 8(a) of the Small Business Act—is a business development program created to help small disadvantaged businesses compete in the marketplace. A certified 8(a) firm is a company owned and operated by socially and economically disadvantaged individuals and eligible to receive federal contracts under the SBA's 8(a) Business Development Program. Suppliers wanting to conduct business with the federal government apply for a designation through the Central Contractor Registration (CCR). Firms that are certified receive assistance and counseling in a structured developmental process over a nine-year period. Maintaining this classification requires an annual review.

SBA has established numerical definitions, called "size standards," for every private sector industry in the U.S. economy; the North American Industry Classification System (NAICS) is used to identify the industries. An industry is coded with a six-digit number, such as 541330 for Engineering Services. A size standard, which is usually stated in number of employees or average annual receipts, represents the largest size that a business (including its subsidiaries and affiliates) may be to remain classified as a small business for SBA and federal contracting programs. All federal agencies must use SBA size standards for contracts identified as small business.

Table 9.1 shows the most commonly used size standards within an NAICS industry sector. If the size of a business exceeds the size standard for its overall industry sector, it may still be a small business for the specific six-digit NAICS industry. Some industries have higher size standards than the general one for the industry group. SBA's Table of Small Business Size Standards lists size standards by six-digit NAICS industry codes.

TABLE 9.1 A Sampling of Small Business Size Standards

NAICS U.S. Industry Title	Size Standards
Construction: General building and heavy construction contractors	$33.5 million
Manufacturing: 75% of industries	500 employees
Mining	500 employees
Retail trade	$7 million
Services: Most common, other than ...	$7 million
—Computer programming, data processing, and systems design	$25 million
Wholesale trade: Small business federal contracts	100 employees

Source: United States Small Business Administration.

Other definitions provided by the SBA include the following:

- A *woman-owned business* is defined as a business that is owned and controlled 51 percent or more by a woman or women. Currently, a woman-owned certification process is not required for federal contracts.
- A *veteran-owned business* is defined as a business that is owned 51 percent by a veteran(s). There is no veteran-owned certification process to complete; self-certification is sufficient.
- A *service-disabled business* is defined as a business that is owned 51 percent by one or more service-disabled veterans. The Veterans Administration confirms service-related disability.
- A *HUBZone business* is defined as a business located in a Historically Underutilized Business Zone, generally areas that are economically disadvantaged. SBA's HUBZone Program is designed to promote economic development and employment growth in distressed areas by providing access to more federal contracting opportunities. Certified small business firms have the opportunity to negotiate contracts and participate in restricted competition limited to HUBZone firms.

THE NATIONAL MINORITY SUPPLIER DEVELOPMENT COUNCIL NMSDC has standardized procedures to ensure consistent and identical review and certification of minority-owned businesses.

A minority-owned business is a for-profit enterprise, regardless of size, physically located in the United States or its trust territories, which is owned, operated and controlled by minority group members.

"Minority group members" are United States citizens who are Asian (Asian Pacific and Asian-Indian), Black, Hispanic and Native American

with at least 25% minimum (documentation to support claim of 25% required from applicant).

Ownership by minority individuals means the business is at least 51% owned by such individuals or, in the case of a publicly-owned business, at least 51% of the stock is owned by one or more such individuals. Further, the management and daily operations are controlled by those minority group members.

> —Minority and Women Business Enterprises, "Certification Overview," www.mwbe.com/cert/certification.htm.

Note that in these terms, *Asian-Indian American* refers to a U.S. citizen whose origins are from India, Pakistan, and Bangladesh. *Asian-Pacific American* refers to a U.S. citizen whose origins are from Japan, China, Taiwan, Korea, Vietnam, Laos, Cambodia, the Philippines, Samoa, Guam, the U.S. Trust Territories of the Pacific, or the Northern Marianas. *American Indian* refers to a person who is a Native American Indian, Eskimo, Aleut, or Native Hawaiian, and regarded as such by the community of which the person claims to be a part. Native Americans must be documented members of a North American tribe, band, or otherwise organized group of native people who are indigenous to the continental United States and proof can be provided through a Native American Blood Degree Certificate (i.e., tribal registry letter, tribal roll register number).

The Business Case for Diversity

The Chubb Group of Insurance Companies states its business case for diversity (on its web site) with elegant simplicity:

> *Those who perceive diversity as exclusively a moral imperative or societal goal are missing the larger point. Workforce diversity needs to be viewed as a competitive advantage and a business opportunity. That's why Chubb makes diversity a business priority and strives to achieve a fully inclusive diverse workforce.*

Many other organizations echo this concept. For example, Sears Holdings' diversity statement, posted on its web site, includes this:

> *Sears Holdings endeavors to provide minority, women, small, HUBZone, veteran or service-disabled veteran businesses with the maximum opportunities to participate as suppliers and contractors for merchandise, supplies and services used in all Sears Holdings business units.*

We recognize that supplier diversity adds value to our business. A diverse supplier base stimulates growth in our communities while helping us bring a wide variety of diverse merchandise and services to our customers.

Thus it is clear that while organizations sincerely acknowledge the "moral imperative" to engage diversity in their supply bases, they also seek to create a competitive advantage and business opportunity by doing so.

Objectives

The key objective in conducting a supplier diversity program is to source, qualify, and purchase from small, disadvantaged businesses. As noted, organizations do so in their own self-interest in order to create opportunity for groups that are historically underrepresented, increasing their economic viability and thereby helping to create new markets for their sponsoring organizations. Businesses also hope to benefit through an increased market share within multicultural and disadvantaged communities. There is also the important consideration that companies doing business with most U.S. and local government entities are evaluated on their ability to contract with diversity enterprises for a measurable portion of their supplies and services. Typically, this requirement is mandated by law.

Measuring Success

To be fully effective, a supplier diversity program must have measurable goals. Measurable goals communicate the program's expectation and provide a framework to measure progress. Typically, goals are established in the strategic planning process for the sourcing organization. These goals should include implementation timetables as well as quantitative goals, such as annual purchase dollars, percent of total purchases, and the number of diversity suppliers doing business with or contracted with.

The NMSDC suggests establishing these measurable goals:

- Performance milestones or in-process review/benchmarks to ensure that adequate bidding opportunities are offered to MBEs
- Quantitative goals that reflect the corporation's use of minority suppliers/contractors (i.e., annual purchase dollars, percent increase over previous year purchases, percent of total purchase value, etc.)
- Qualitative goals that reflect progress in implementing specific minority business development strategies (i.e., mentoring, joint venturing, strategic alliances, education, financial assistance, etc.)

Supplier Diversity Best Practices

Recognized best practices maintain that organizations should have and adhere to a diversity *business development policy statement* that is signed by the chief executive officer (CEO). This policy statement should guide sourcing operations and should be a requirement in the sourcing and contracting process. Best practices also include a contract flow-down clause requiring the implementation of similar policies by the supplier in its sourcing and contracting activities.

Best practices suggest that organizations should demonstrate a number of specific characteristics in its diversity programs. As stated by NMSDC, this includes:

- *Commitment on the part of the chief executive officer and his/her senior officers*
- *A minority business development director specifically assigned the responsibility for implementing the program*
- *Minority business development goals that are established and monitored the same as other corporate goals and objectives*
- *A corporate culture which promotes innovative techniques to develop minority businesses*

To undertake a minority business development program without making it a part of the day-to-day business of the organization is to condemn it to almost certain failure. But by careful planning, policy formation, goal setting, implementation, monitoring and accountability, the program can reach its goals and produce significant benefits for the corporation and the community.

Like all corporate policies, a minority business development policy must have the backing of the senior line officers if it is to be implemented effectively throughout the organization. Through written and verbal communication, the CEO should emphasize to senior officers that purchasing from minority businesses is beneficial to the company in many ways.

Support for Diversity Suppliers

Establishing programs that support diversity supplier development should not end (as it too often does) with just a policy statement; much more is needed. There are many ways to support the diversity supplier community through business mentoring and inclusion in the organization's processes:

- **Financial assistance.** Funding is possibly the single most critical issue that SDBs must deal with. The buying organization can offer substantial assistance in getting working capital by issuing advance purchase orders that the supplier can use to obtain funding. The organization may also consider providing equity, loan guarantees, or even financing loans itself. In fact, some organizations have actually hosted its developing suppliers as a form of incubator, providing facilities and administrative support at low or no cost.
- **Training and mentoring.** This area includes support through inclusion in organizational training programs, especially those encompassing management training, business planning, human resources, finance and managing cash flow, sourcing and procurement methods, and so on.

  Organizations can also assist their diversity suppliers by helping them to identify areas where they are deficient and where training may be required—perhaps even providing appropriate staff members to conduct the training.
- **Technical assistance.** Buying organizations can provide a number of technical services, from engineering development to establishing a quality control function. Technical assistance can be provided in the form of low-cost technical services and assistance with product development, among other things.
- **Registration.** Organizations with viable supplier diversity programs provide Internet access to their programs and a means of Internet-accessible registration to incorporate those firms registered in a sourcing database. Often this is a simple process that requires little more than identification of the supplier, its diversity category, and the products or services that it provides. The database is searchable by the sourcing and the procurement groups.

Other Best Practice Elements

There are a number of other elements you may want to consider applying to diversity sourcing operations. These will include:

- Integrating supplier diversity goals and strategic plans
- Establishing annual goals for purchases from diversity suppliers and developing mechanisms to track diversity spending
- Achievement of annual diversity sourcing goals included in individual performance measures and tied to compensation
- Incorporating the consideration of diversity suppliers as a standard element in the sourcing process

- Educating internal customers on the benefits of diversity sourcing; providing training for using groups, sourcing, and procurement personnel
- Developing outreach and communications programs to attract potential diversity suppliers to register for solicitation opportunities, including information on the organization's web site outlining the sourcing program for diversity suppliers
- Active participation by the senior sourcing manager in diversity councils
- Creating an internal supplier diversity council to help guide diversity program policy
- Incorporating flow-down provisions in contracts encouraging the use of second-tier diversity suppliers with specific goals
- Requiring prime (first-tier) suppliers to report on second-tier outreach metrics and progress to goals using a supplier portal
- Rewarding diversity suppliers that demonstrate innovation with an outlet for their ideas, especially seeking to adopt breakthrough innovation in supply management
- Holding business and technology road map workshops for the small businesses that have been engaged by your organization; providing the opportunity to exchange innovative ideas and plans for the next time period (e.g., month, year, etc.) so that your organization and its suppliers can synchronize collaborative efforts
- Encouraging and supporting continuous improvement processes in the diversity supply base
- Paying less attention to total spend with diversity suppliers and more attention to how that spend is distributed, as illustrated in the next example

Spread

- How many diverse companies are participating in the organization's total spend?
- The Top 500 diverse-owned companies have over $53 billion in annual revenue that represent over 50 percent of all reported diverse spend.

What Has the Greatest Impact?

- A $50 million contact to one company
- 50 $1 million contracts to companies in one geographic area

Visit www.DiversityBusiness.com for a list of the top 500 diversity suppliers.

Source: DiversityBusiness.com, "Fortune 500 Diversity Procurement," www .diversitybusiness.com/news/diversity.magazine/99200849.asp.

Global Supplier Diversity

As we have pointed out, supplier diversity programs are developed to create equal social and economic opportunity for classes of SDBs. The current approach has proven very effective in the United States with many government organizations (federal, state, county, and city) and their suppliers meeting their objectives on a continuing basis. Can this process be extended globally?

Many U.S. organizations doing business in multinational environments have initiated programs for "Global Diversity." However, we could find no definition of the term and note that many companies carry over the same U.S. language used for supplier diversity. This is likely a good start, but it's difficult, we feel, to apply U.S. criteria directly to international conditions. Sourcing from different global cultures and countries can serve as a form of supplier diversity. However, simply combining the term "diversity" with "global sourcing" can be misleading and confusing.

Our Definition of Global Supplier Diversity

Consequently, in promoting a global philosophy of economic inclusion—that is, enabling all business organizations to freely and equally engage in commercial activities within their scope—it seems appropriate to have a formal definition. We propose this:

Global Supplier Diversity (GSD) is a formal program actively engaged in by a buying organization to support and encourage the development of small businesses owned by members of economically disadvantaged groups within a country or defined geographical area.

GSD is sustained through the award of business, mentoring, and technical and financial assistance consistent with the culture and legal requirements in which the supplier operates.

An economically disadvantaged, diversity small business is one without equal access to business opportunities as a result of the ethnic, social, religious, disabled, or gender status of its owner.

A small business is defined as one with fewer than 250 employees and gross income below $1 million per year.

This definition enables the business organization to operate its program within the scope of supplier diversity principles already in existence in the United States but with activities specific to the country or geographical area in which it is conducting business.

Some Encouraging Efforts

One very significant effort is being made by a number of companies that have been collaborating to develop a workable program. Cisco is a founder and sponsor of the Minority Supplier Diversity China (MSD China) organization, a nonprofit set up to help the development of China's minority-owned businesses by connecting minority suppliers to various companies as a means of providing procurement opportunities.

Significantly, participants in the MSD program include Dell, IBM, Motorola, Intel, Boeing, Johnson Controls, Coca-Cola, ITT, Tianjin Tasly Group, MSD China, PepsiCo, Wyndham, and Delphi. The effort also appears to have Chinese government support, so it should be possible to use the project as a model to assist those wanting to initiate a similar program for SDBs in other countries.

Through its program, MSD China has identified 55 ethnic minority groups in China that would be able to benefit from an organized effort to foster diversity; it has established a permanent operating organization and developed a number of outreach programs.

Unfortunately, Global Supplier Diversity is an exception rather than a common situation. We found few U.S. businesses that have an international supplier diversity program as advanced as Cisco's.

Diversity Advocacy Organizations

In the United States, a number of organizations, both private and public, advocate and support programs focused on SDBs. A number of these organizations provide certification/verification of the status of the applicant company, which for many diversity suppliers is the first step toward establishing themselves as eligible for future business as a member of this business category.

Verification Organizations

Here is a sampling of certification and support organizations that can be accessed through the Web:

- **Central Contractor Registration (CCR):** www.bpn.gov/ccr. "The primary registrant database for the U.S. Federal Government. CCR collects, validates, stores and disseminates data in support of agency acquisition missions."
- **HUBZone Certification:** www.sba.gov/hubzone. "It is our mission to promote job growth, capital investment, and economic development

to historically underutilized business zones, referred to as HUBZones, by providing contracting assistance to small businesses located in these economically distressed communities."

- **National Gay and Lesbian Chamber of Commerce (NGLCC):** www .nglcc.org. "The NGLCC is the business advocate and direct link between lesbian, gay, bisexual and transgender (LGBT) business owners, corporations, and government, representing the interests of more than 1.4 million LGBT businesses and entrepreneurs. The NGLCC is committed to forming a broad-based coalition of LGBT owned and friendly businesses, professionals, and major corporations for the purpose of promoting economic growth and the prosperity of our members."

- **National Minority Supplier Development Council:** www.nmsdc .org. The NMSDC "provides a direct link between corporate America and minority-owned businesses. NMSDC is one of the country's leading business membership organizations. It was chartered in 1972 to provide increased procurement and business opportunities for minority businesses of all sizes."

- **U.S. Small Business Administration:** www.sba.gov/index.html. "The U.S. Small Business Administration (SBA) was created in 1953 as an independent agency of the federal government to aid, counsel, assist and protect the interests of small business concerns, to preserve free competitive enterprise and to maintain and strengthen the overall economy of our nation."

- **VetBIZ:** www.vetbiz.gov. VetBIZ is a Web portal provided by the U.S. Department of Veteran Affairs as The Center of Veterans Enterprise. "Verification of Veteran-Owned and Service-Disabled Veteran-Owned Small Businesses per Public Law (P.L.) 109-461."

- **Women's Business Enterprise National Council (WBENC):** www .wbenc.org. "The Women's Business Enterprise National Council (WBENC), founded in 1997, is the largest third-party certifier of businesses owned controlled, and operated by women in the United States. WBENC, a national 501(c)(3) non-profit, partners with 14 Regional Partner Organizations to provide its national standard of certification to women-owned businesses throughout the country. WBENC is also the nation's leading advocate of women-owned businesses as suppliers to America's corporations."

Other Support Organizations

In addition to the certification/verification organizations, there are a number of other support groups. Here is just a small sampling of them:

- **Association of Latino Professionals in Finance and Accounting (ALPFA):** www.alpfa.org. ALPFA is the premier Latino organization for professionals and students in business, finance, accounting, and related professions. ALPFA has active members, committed business partners, and quality programs.
- **American Indian Business Leaders (AIBL):** www.aibl.org/home. The AIBL is the only American Indian nonprofit organization solely dedicated to empowering business students in the United States. Its programs are designed to engage students in activities that stimulate, enhance, and expand educational experiences beyond traditional academic methods. All students are encouraged to participate in AIBL regardless of race, academic major, or career objectives.
- **Association of MultiEthnic Americans (AMEA):** www.ameasite.org. This international nonprofit association of organizations is dedicated to advocacy, education, and collaboration on behalf of the multiethnic, multiracial, and transracial adoption community.
- **Center for Advancement of Racial and Ethnic Equity, American Council on Education (ACE):** www.acenet.edu/Content/ NavigationMenu/ProgramsServices/CAREE/index.htm. This center monitors and reports on the progress of African Americans, Latinos, Asian Americans, and American Indians in postsecondary education and works to improve their educational and employment opportunities in higher education.
- **Disability.Gov:** www.disability.gov. This web site is an online guide to the federal government's disability-related information and resources.
- **DiversityInc:** www.diversityinc.com. "[T]he leading publication on diversity and business. DiversityInc's CEO and owner is Luke Visconti. DiversityInc was founded in 1998 as a web-based publication; our print magazine was launched in 2002. We reach more than 1 million unique monthly visitors on DiversityInc.com, and the magazine has circulation of over 340,000. DiversityInc.com has the largest dedicated career center for diverse professionals."
- **Foundation for Ethnic Understanding:** www.ffeu.org/index.htm. A national nonprofit "dedicated to strengthening relations between ethnic communities." The foundation's work focuses primarily on Black-Jewish relations but has recently expanded to include Latino-Jewish relations.
- **Minority Professional Network:** www.minorityprofessionalnetwork .com/nonprofit.asp. "The Global Career, Economic and Lifestyle Connection for Progressive Professionals" is a connection for progressive multicultural professionals. It offers robust online, e-marketing, and offline branding; recruiting; event support; training; and related advertising and outreach solutions.

- **The Multicultural Advantage:** www.multiculturaladvantage.com. "An information site with articles, job opportunities, event listings, research tool, downloads, links and other resources for professionals from diverse background. The site also addresses the needs of diversity recruiting and workplace diversity professionals who are seeking to reach and understand them."
- **National Black MBA Association (NBMBAA):** www.nbmbaa.org. This organization is dedicated to developing partnerships that result in the creation intellectual and economic wealth in the Black community. In partnership with over 400 of the top U.S. business organizations, the association has inroads into a wide range of industries as well as the public and private sector.
- **National MultiCultural Institute:** www.nmci.org. Founded in 1983, the National MultiCultural Institute (NMCI) is "proud to be one of the first organizations to have recognized the nation's need for new services, knowledge, and skills in the growing field of multiculturalism and diversity."
- **Workforce Diversity Network (WDN):** www.workforcediversity network.com. This organization "is the nation's leading network of professionals and organizations dedicated to professional development, understanding, promotion and management of diversity as an essential part of business success."

Summary

In this chapter, we examined the nature of supplier diversity programs beginning with definitions and the process of certification. We then looked at making a business case for diversity and how some organizations have approached the process. From there, we covered supplier diversity best practices, including the types of support available to diversity suppliers and a number of other best practice elements.

We concluded with a discussion of the status of global supplier diversity, our own definition, and an extensive listing of organizations providing certification and support to diversity suppliers.

CHAPTER 10

Sustainability

By now it is clear to almost everyone that the Earth is facing some very significant environmental challenges, considered by most to be the result of human activity and waste. We somehow need to reverse these trends so that available resources, including the very air we breathe and the water we drink, are available to future generations. We call this concept "sustainability."

The Institute for Supply Management defines the term on its web site as follows:

> *Sustainability is the ability to meet current needs without hindering the ability to meet the needs of future generations in terms of economic, environmental and social challenges.*

The philosophy of sustainability revolves around the general concepts of social responsibility, in terms of how we use our earthly resources. In supply management, we have simplified the term for this philosophy as "green sourcing."

Sustainability requires commitment by management and employees alike. New global and national standards for socially responsible and environmentally sound practices are continually being developed. To maintain effectiveness, organizations must constantly adapt and stay a step or two ahead of the changing dynamics.

It is very difficult to identify best practices that are themselves sustainable. But clearly it is still in every organization's best interests to review its operations and determine what can be done to meet the current demands of its industry, its business partners, and its shareholders.

In this chapter, we examine the important areas to consider when sourcing to embrace principles of sustainability and, to the extent that we have clear data, what is being done to address this area of concern.

Issues in Sustainability

Social responsibility and environmental concerns impact the process of sourcing in numerous areas, and each of them has a somewhat varied set of challenges. In general, however, we can identify three specific areas where issues in the commercial sphere are abundant:

1. **Materials.** Issues concern eliminating waste, recycling materials, reducing the rates of natural resource depletion, including food, and eliminating the dangers of hazardous materials and the effects of natural disasters created by humankind.
2. **Toxic discharge.** Issues relating to poor air quality are associated with greenhouse gases, ozone depletion, and air pollutants as these elements relate to global climate warming. We must also consider waste discharge into waterways and water table contamination. Universal waste reduction programs are currently characterized by an astounding lack of action and the petty bickering from nation to nation.
3. **Energy consumption.** Here the issues revolve around finding alternatives sources of energy to replace unsustainable fuel sources, such as oil, coal, and gas. These are issues faced primarily by the developed (and to some extent, developing) countries.

As we go forward with our examination of sustainability, we will review each of these areas in more depth as they apply to global sourcing and effective supplier management. Since our examination provides an overview rather than a detailed analysis of specific initiatives, we will maintain a broad view and not examine local initiatives.

Materials

As previously noted, there are a substantial number of environmental issues relating to how we use materials. Achieving sustainability in our current business and governmental environment appears to be largely a matter of customer demand, so the sourcing team can have a significant impact by establishing or adhering to relevant environmental standards.

WASTE AND WASTE REDUCTION The reduction of waste in all forms is central to sustainability. Unfortunately, there is no universal standard for either defining waste or reducing waste, although countless initiatives exist at regional, national, local, corporate, and even personal levels.

Waste, in many circumstances, can be difficult to identify. The European Union (EU) defines the term in Directive 2008/98/EC as follows: "'waste' means any substance or object which the holder discards or intends or is required to discard." This definition includes solid waste, liquid waste, and airborne waste. We can also apply the term "waste" to scrap and rework common to manufacturing industries. Today, most waste is disposed of in landfills, through incineration, or in oceans and waterways.

Recycling is the most widely used tool used to reduce waste, followed by reduced consumption and detoxification of airborne and liquid waste streams. Here, too, governments (at all levels) and various industries have developed their own sets of standards and reduction goals, so it's quite difficult to determine a standard for reduction goals. For the purposes of sourcing, it will be necessary to determine the amount of a supplier's current waste stream and decide if its goals for reduction are in line with its industry standards or your own organization's goals. Later in this chapter, we review the International Organization for Standardization (ISO) environmental standards and the United Nations' Global Compact.

In terms of waste reduction *processes*, the EU, while it fails to state measurable objectives, offers this set of instructive guidelines (http://ec.europa .eu/environment/waste/index.htm):

The European Union's approach to waste management is based on three principles:

1. **Waste prevention:** *This is a key factor in any waste management strategy. If we can reduce the amount of waste generated in the first place and reduce its hazardousness by reducing the presence of dangerous substances in products, then disposing of it will automatically become simpler. Waste prevention is closely linked with improving manufacturing methods and influencing consumers to demand greener products and less packaging.*
2. **Recycling and reuse:** *If waste cannot be prevented, as many of the materials as possible should be recovered, preferably by recycling. The European Commission has defined several specific "waste streams" for priority attention, the aim being to reduce their overall environmental impact. This includes packaging waste, end-of-life vehicles, batteries, electrical and electronic waste. EU directives now require Member States to introduce legislation on waste collection, reuse, recycling and disposal of these waste streams. Several EU countries are already managing to recycle over 50% of packaging waste.*
3. **Improving final disposal and monitoring:** *Where possible, waste that cannot be recycled or reused should be safely incinerated, with landfill only used as a last resort. Both these methods need close*

monitoring because of their potential for causing severe environmental damage. The EU has recently approved a directive setting strict guidelines for landfill management. It bans certain types of waste, such as used tyres, and sets targets for reducing quantities of biodegradable rubbish. Another recent directive lays down tough limits on emission levels from incinerators. The Union also wants to reduce emissions of dioxins and acid gases such as nitrogen oxides (NO_x), sulfur dioxides (SO_2), and hydrogen chlorides (HCL), which can be harmful to human health.

RENEWABLE RESOURCES AND HABITATS Renewable resources are those that are replaced by natural processes faster than they are consumed or destroyed through human activity. Renewability (or sustainability) is a major area of concern since many of our natural resources and areas of wildlife habitats are rapidly disappearing. To maintain sustainability, the guiding principles are those of long-term conservation that ensures the environment is able maintain its supply of the materials necessary to sustain life.

Resources Typical renewable resources that we depend on, and that are currently threatened, include a number of commodities, such as forest products, agricultural products, potable water, soil, marine species, and biomass. Also included on our list are some renewable resources that are not inherently threatened, such as wind power and solar energy.

We must also closely consider the use of nonrenewable resources—those that are not being replaced as they are consumed—such as oil, coal, and gas. Sourcing professionals must assess their suppliers' use of these elements along with their efforts to replace them with renewable sources. Again, unfortunately, there are no global standards for slowing the depletion of natural resources.

Habitat In addition to sustaining wildlife, natural habitats are an important form of resources for humans as well. Many environmentalists believe that we can maintain a natural balance on Earth only if existing species are able to survive so that we can maintain our system of biodiversity. They believe that globally, we are inextricably linked to the well-being and continuation of diverse species.

We know, too, that the disappearance of jungle and forest lands will have an adverse effect on our quality of life since the forests' greenery replaces harmful carbon dioxide with the oxygen that we need to breathe.

HAZARDOUS MATERIALS Definitions of "hazardous materials" abound, but collectively they describe the same concept: any substance or compound that has the capability of producing adverse effects on the health and safety

Forest Depletion

One lumber buyer we know tells us that in the 1960s and 1970s, he would travel to Brazil to select hardwoods, such as the then-popular rosewood. He would fly into Rio, stay the night, and the next morning take a two- to three-hour boat trip to the sawmill.

By 1997, the same trip to the sawmill would take three days: a flight to Rio, an overnight stay, another four-hour flight to a commercial hub, another overnight stay, and then a six- to seven-hour boat ride to the sawmill.

The reason? Forest land has increasingly vanished as a result of clear-cutting for lumber and agriculture and industrial mining.

of human beings. In most parts of the world, the use and disposal of materials that have been classified as hazardous is closely regulated. As a result, sourcing professionals must determine the extent to which their organization and their suppliers are required to comply with existing regulations. Noncompliance increases the risk of supply interruption and extensive liability exposure.

In the United States, a number of regulatory agencies at the federal level, virtually all states, and many local governments have passed regulations restricting the use, transport, and disposal of hazardous materials. Some of the key U.S. agencies requiring regulatory compliance include:

- **Department of Transportation.** DOT regulates the transport and temporary storage of hazardous materials. "The Hazardous Materials Regulations (HMR) are issued by the Pipeline and Hazardous Materials Safety Administration and govern the transportation of hazardous materials by highway, rail, vessel, and air. The HMR address hazardous materials classification, packaging, hazard communication, emergency response information and training." For a list of applicable regulations, see: www.phmsa.dot.gov/hazmat/regs.
- **Occupational Safety and Health Administration (OSHA).** In addition to the DOT, the U.S. Department of Labor maintains a listing of the standards set forth by federal regulation.

  In order to ensure chemical safety in the workplace, information must be available about the identities and hazards of the chemicals. OSHA's Hazard Communication Standard requires the development and dissemination of such information:

- Chemical manufacturers and importers are required to evaluate the hazards of the chemicals they produce or import, and prepare labels and Material Safety Data Sheets (MSDSs) to convey the hazard information to their downstream customers.
- Any employer with hazardous chemicals in its workplace must have labels and MSDSs for exposed workers and must train them to handle the chemicals appropriately.

An extensive list of the standards for hazardous materials in the workplace can be found on OSHA's web site: www.osha.gov/dsg/hazcom/index.html.

- **Environmental Protection Agency (EPA).** The EPA is primarily concerned with the handling and disposal of hazardous waste. It defines hazardous waste in these terms:

> *Hazardous waste is waste that is dangerous or potentially harmful to our health or the environment. Hazardous wastes can be liquids, solids, gases, or sludges. They can be discarded commercial products, like cleaning fluids or pesticides, or the by-products of manufacturing processes.*

You can find a list of important references, including materials that are classified as hazardous, on the EPA web site at: www.epa.gov/osw/hazard/index.htm.

Internationally, many sets of regulations exist regarding the transportation of hazardous goods by rail, sea, and road. The United Nations (UN) has developed a set of guidelines for international use (primarily in Europe) that can be accessed here: www.unece.org/trans/danger/publi/manual/Rev4/ManRev4-files_e.html.

The UN has also developed a set of model regulations to be used as a further guideline. It can be accessed at: www.unece.org/trans/danger/publi/unrec/rev15/15files_e.html.

MAN-MADE AND NATURAL DISASTERS The U.S. Department of Health and Human Services (HHS) defines man-made disasters in these terms:

> *Man-made disasters are events which, either intentionally or by accident cause severe threats to public health and well-being. Because their occurrence is unpredictable, man-made disasters pose an especially challenging threat that must be dealt with through vigilance, and proper preparedness and response.*

The HHS listing of man-made disaster categories covers chemical agents, radiation, pandemics, and forms of terrorism. To this list we should add oil and chemical spills and accidental nuclear discharge. Perhaps even more significantly, we should include wars and other armed conflicts.

HHS also defines and tracks major natural disasters such as earthquake, fire or wildfire, flood and dam failure, hurricane and high wind, landslide, thunderstorm, tornadoes, tsunami, volcano, extreme cold, and extreme heat. To this list we can add avalanches, mud slides, and blizzards.

Suppliers located in areas prone to these events have a much higher risk of operational interruptions and therefore must have contingency plans in place. If you are sourcing in these areas, you should put in place a contingency plan for what to do should a supplier experience a work stoppage due to one of these events.

Toxic Discharge

We discussed toxic discharges to some extent in the preceding section. However, a number of other factors that affect the environment were not discussed. Importantly, these other factors also relate to the very important concerns regarding global warming and ongoing sources of environmental pollution.

GREENHOUSE GASES So much has been written about global warming and the effect of greenhouse gases that adding to the topic seems unnecessary. "Global warming" is the term most commonly used to describe the gradual warming up of Earth's atmosphere as a result of increased greenhouse gas emissions.

From a sourcing perspective, you must be alert to any potential toxic discharge generated by a supplier, including gases that help create the greenhouse warming effect. Where potential for discharge exists, risk increases exponentially and should be included in your supplier selection decision criteria. Despite the current international bickering over quotas for carbon emissions, limitations will eventually find universal adoption.

CARBON FOOTPRINTS AND CARBON DIOXIDE REDUCTION Scientists for the most part agree that the key to reversing the global warming trend that threatens our extinction is to reduce so-called greenhouse gases. A primary greenhouse gas has been identified as carbon dioxide (CO_2), and its emission is known as a "carbon footprint." This is a measure of the amount of greenhouse gases produced through burning fossil fuels and other human activities, converted to tons of CO_2 equivalent that we individually produce. You can calculate any carbon footprint by visiting this (or a similar) site: www.carbonfootprint.com/calculator.aspx.

Carbon management has recently taken the form of cap-and-trade legislation. This is a market-based system whereby companies are provided with a quota based on a calculated baseline from which they can sell or buy emission credits depending on their usage. In the case of the EU Emission Trading System, which is reported to cover more than 10,000 installations, large organizations are required to monitor their carbon emissions and provide reductions according to a rather complex, country-by-country reduction plan. Similar legislation is in process for the United States and other countries in accordance with the 1992 United Nations' Framework Convention on Climate Change or the Kyoto Protocol.

What is potentially significant for sourcing activities in this process is that emissions footprints may be tied to an organization's entire supply chain. Largely, this footprint will be calculated on the basis of shipment size and mileage. Since truck transportation accounts for a very significant portion of carbon emissions, there are currently a plethora of new software applications designed to calculate the truck transportation footprint and suggest possible methods for reducing it. One possible reduction method would be to switch from truck to rail transport, which, per unit, has a significantly lower footprint. Another method might be to switch to local production to reduce the need for lengthy transportation and/or to switch to other energy sources that have lower emissions.

Another proposed method is a straightforward carbon tax. The Carbon Tax Center regards this method as more predictable and having less impact on pricing. You can find a more detailed discussion at the center's site, www.carbontax.org.

Interestingly, the U.S. Environmental Protection Agency has been working in the background for a number of years to develop methods for the reduction of greenhouse gases in general. If you recall, it was the EPA that led the initiatives for the reduction of acid rain emissions.

An outline of the EPA's WARM system, which provides a method for calculating the overall emission of greenhouse gases including methane and nitrous oxide and other greenhouse gases rather than just carbon alone, is presented next.

U.S. Waste and Emissions Initiative

EPA created the WAste Reduction Model (WARM) to help solid waste planners and organizations track and voluntarily report greenhouse gas emissions reductions from several different waste management practices. WARM is available both as a Web-based calculator and as a Microsoft Excel spreadsheet (355K WinZip archive).

WARM calculates and totals GHG [greenhouse gas] emissions of baseline and alternative waste management practices—source reduction, recycling, combustion, composting, and land-filling. The model calculates emissions in metric tons of carbon equivalent (MTCE), metric tons of carbon dioxide equivalent (MTCO$_2$E), and energy units (million BTU) across a wide range of material types commonly found in municipal solid waste (MSW).

WARM is periodically updated as new information becomes available and new material types are added. Users may refer to the model history to better understand the differences among various versions of WARM. WARM was last updated in November, 2009.

Source: U.S. Environmental Protection Agency, "WAste Reduction Model," August 2010, www.epa.gov/climatechange/wycd/waste/calculators/ Warm_home.html.

OZONE DEPLETION Earth's ozone layer (in the stratosphere) protects us from harmful ultraviolet rays generated by the sun by providing a natural filter. It has been thinning at an accelerated rate, and the "holes" in the ozone layer around the polar regions have been growing larger. In simple terms, ozone depletion is the result of emissions of chlorofluorocarbon compounds called freons and bromofluorocarbon compounds called halons at the Earth's surface.

Ozone depletion has been identified as the major contributor to climate change. "Climate change" is the term used to describe how the weather and climate patterns are changing as a result of global warming. To simplify: Global warming and ozone depletion both contribute to climate change.

POLLUTION In addition to global warming and climate change, sustainability in the supply chain also includes eliminating other sources of environmental pollution, including air pollution, water pollution, and ground contamination. In these areas, numerous global initiatives are under way to eliminate waste at its source through the use of nontoxic substances, modification of production processes, conservation methods, and recycling. The elimination of waste of all types has long been a recognized factor in cost reduction and improved manufacturing productivity since the introduction of Just-in-Time concepts in the late 1950s.

Worldwide, there are several treaties and regulations aimed at reducing the amount of waste that contributes to pollution. In the United States, the

Pollution Prevention Act of 1990 seeks to establish a collaborative effort with industry and the EPA. The goal of this legislation is to reduce pollution at its source. Although compliance is currently voluntary, the act creates the potential for a future enforcement-oriented attack by the government in its efforts at pollution prevention.

The EPA's approach establishes reduction of pollution at its source as the most effective approach, with recycling and treatment following. The EPA (at www.epa.gov/gcc/pubs/pgcc/presgcc.html) defines source reduction as any practice that:

- *Reduces the amount of any hazardous substance, pollutant, or contaminant entering any waste stream or otherwise released into the environment (including fugitive emissions) prior to recycling, treatment, or disposal; and*
- *Reduces the hazards to public health and the environment associated with the release of such substances, pollutants, or contaminants.*

Reduction practices that are emphasized include modifications to equipment, processes and procedures, product design and modifications, substitution of materials, and better housekeeping.

Energy Consumption

Sustainability also encompasses the use of renewable energy sources—those that cannot be depleted, such as wind power, solar energy, hydropower, geothermal energy, nuclear energy, hydrogen fuel cells, biologically based sources, and other natural resources. Sustainability is a high priority for many governments and industries, considering that the world's current reliance on fossil fuels (petroleum) will not be sustainable much past midcentury at the current rate of consumption. However, many of these sources require significant investments in order to convert from today's oil-based processes to efficient renewable energy. While the development of these sources is clearly under way, it has not reached the point where it is practical in most situations and where it can be legislatively mandated.

The dilemma for the sourcing team, then, is how to evaluate compliance with the use of renewable energy sources when virtually no standards or requirements exist. Most of the initiatives we see in the United States are directed toward existing power suppliers, requiring that a percentage of their energy come from renewable sources. These are called renewable portfolio standards and have been established in the United States by a majority of states. The problem is that they are focused on the most cost-efficient methods, such as wind and methane from landfills, but fail to provide adequate support for smaller-scale methods, such as solar energy, largely due to cost considerations.

The recent "Enterprise Renewable Energy Adoption Survey," conducted by the *Environmental Leader* and *Retailer Daily* and available at https://reports.environmentalleader.com, found that:

> *Of all the varying factors that go into an enterprise's decision to enact a renewable energy programme—brand image, corporate responsibility, and future viability of fossil fuel—finance is the most important of all, as would be expected of a business decision.*

> *In virtually every question asking respondents why they did (or did not) make a certain decision regarding a renewable energy implementation, a financial consideration was the top answer. This applies whether respondents purchase renewable energy from a third party, RECs, or generate their own renewable energy on site. It also applies to respondents who have not yet implemented renewable energy, whether they plan to in the future or not.*

Guidelines

Many global initiatives are currently underway that seek to remedy the issues in sustainability. It is incumbent on the sourcing team leader to determine which ones may apply to its suppliers and the extent to which each supplier is in compliance. The task will not be easy, as there are so many government and industry standards. To further complicate matters, many of these standards are still in their early stages and will continue evolving. Reviewed here are two key sets of guidelines that comprehensively address sustainability.

ISO 14001 Guidelines

ISO 14001 (and its update, ISO 14001:2004) sets out requirements for an Environmental Management System (EMS) that can be used by an organization to measure and document its environmental compliance. The key advantage to looking for ISO environmental requirements is that compliance can be externally audited and certified by an accredited certification body. In fact, there are a number of tools available for organizations (and sourcing teams) to conduct self-assessments to determine if they are compliant and can be certified.

List of ISO 14000 Series Standards

ISO 14001 Environmental Management Systems—Requirements
ISO 14004 Environmental Management Systems—General guidelines
ISO 14015 Environmental Assessment
ISO 14020–14025 Environmental Labels and Declarations
ISO 14031 Environmental Performance Evaluation
ISO 14040–14049 Life Cycle Assessment
ISO 14050 Terms and Definitions
ISO 14062 Improvements to Environmental Impact Goals
ISO 14063 Communication
ISO 14064 Measuring, Quantifying, and Reducing Greenhouse
    Gas Emissions
ISO 19011 Audit Protocol for 14000 and 9000 Series Standards

United Nations Global Compact

Rather than attempt to summarize the UN initiative on supply chain sustainability, due to its importance in defining governing principles of supply chain sustainability, we have printed it here as reference:

Supply Chain Sustainability

Global Compact Launches New Work on Sustainable Supply Chains

The United Nations Global Compact encourages signatories to engage with their suppliers around the Ten Principles, and thereby to develop more sustainable supply chain practices. However, many companies lack the knowledge or capacity to effectively integrate the principles into their existing supply chain programmes and operations. In particular, a challenge remains to ensure that sustainability considerations are embedded within all sourcing processes.

To assist companies in improving their processes, the Global Compact and partners are currently developing guidance on how to take a more proactive approach to integrate the Ten Principles into supply chain management practices. Because supply chain sustainability is a cross-cutting issue, this work is closely coordinated with the strategy and work done in the four Global Compact issues areas (human rights, labour, environment and anti-corruption).

The Global Compact Office has entered into a strategic partnership with BSR (Business for Social Responsibility), a global business membership network and consultancy focused on sustainability, to develop an implementation guide and a learning and assessment tool for Global Compact signatories. This guidance will be launched at the UN Global Compact Leaders Summit 2010, on 24–25 June in New York. . . .

Background

Corporate supply chains have grown in scale and complexity globally over the past decades. Open markets have enabled companies to source from suppliers in developing and emerging economies, or to move or outsource production, because of the cost advantage these regions offer. As a business strategy, this can deliver significant benefits such as reduced costs, and enhanced profitability and shareholder value. At the same time, it can contribute to much needed economic and social development, and higher standards of living for millions of people.

However, widespread concerns about poor social and environmental conditions in companies' supply chains have emerged. Weak implementation of local social and environmental regulation has forced companies to address issues that traditionally have been seen to lie outside of their core competencies and responsibilities.

Moreover, public scrutiny of business behaviour has led to rising expectations that companies are responsible for the environmental, social and governance (ESG) practices of their suppliers. Failure to address suppliers' ESG performance can give rise to significant operational and reputational risks that can threaten to undermine any potential gains from moving into these markets. As a result, a company's overall commitment to corporate citizenship can be seriously discredited if low standards of business conduct are found to persist in their supply chain.

Supply Chain Sustainability

Corporate buying practices can impact suppliers' ability to improve their business conduct. Downward pressure on cost and efficiency can force suppliers to contravene some of their own

(continued)

(*continued*)

ESG standards in order to meet their buyers' commercial require-ments. At the opposite end of the scale, companies can use their purchasing power to help instill good ESG practices in small and medium-sized companies across the developing world.

Today, successful supply chain managers must increasingly think beyond short-term financial considerations to building relation-ships that can deliver long-term value along the entire supply chain. This includes incorporating sustainability issues into the company's sourcing and purchasing practices. In fact, companies that do engage with their suppliers around these issues consti-tute one of the most important drivers for spreading corporate citizenship principles around the world.

The Business Case

Incorporating environmental, social and governance consider-ations into supply chain management can deliver a range of business benefits:

- *Risks are better anticipated and managed (risk is spread out across different players)*
- *Reduced operational risks such as disruption to supply, increased cost and lack of access to key raw materials*
- *"Informal" or "social" license to operate within communi-ties, legal systems and governments that otherwise might be antagonistic*
- *Reduced costs and enhanced efficiency and productivity*
- *Improved working conditions can reduce turnover and improve quality and reliability*
- *Environmental responsibility improves efficiency and prof-itability*
- *Corporate brand and values, and customer and consumer confidence and loyalty are protected and enhanced*
- *Process and product innovation. Empowered suppliers uncover opportunities for developing sustainable products and services*
- *Examples from leading companies show that good supply chain management can increase shareholder value*

Source: United Nations, "Supply Chain Sustainability," March 16, 2010, www.unglobalcompact.org/Issues/supply_chain/index.html.

Lean Six Sigma

Six Sigma uses statistical methods to systemically analyze manufacturing processes in order to reduce process variation and is often used to support continual improvement activities. It is being used by some companies to assess areas of waste to which lean methods (practices that seek to reduce all forms of waste) can be applied as solutions.

The EPA (at www.epa.gov/lean/thinking/sixsigma.htm) describes the potential benefits of applying Six Sigma processes to waste reduction in this way:

> *By removing variation from production processes, fewer defects inherently result. A reduction in defects can, in turn, help eliminate waste from processes in three fundamental ways:*
>
> 1. *Fewer defects decreases the number of products that must be scrapped;*
> 2. *Fewer defects also means that the raw materials, energy, and resulting waste associated with the scrap are eliminated;*
> 3. *Fewer defects decrease the amount of energy, raw material, and wastes that are used or generated to fix defective products that can be re-worked.*

> *Six Sigma tools can help focus attention on reducing conditions that can result in accidents, spills, and equipment malfunctions. This can reduce the solid and hazardous wastes (e.g., contaminated rags and adsorbent pads) resulting from spills and leaks and their clean-up.*

> *Six Sigma techniques that focus on product durability and reliability can increase the lifespan of products. This can reduce the frequency with which the product will need to be replaced, reducing the overall environmental impacts associated with meeting the customer need.*

Criteria for Supplier Evaluation

As noted in earlier chapters, supplier evaluation is generally best tailored to a specific organization and a specific requirement. However, if you are considering evaluating sustainability as part of your supplier selection criteria for the first time and would like a starting point, please consider including these elements in your solicitation:

- Do you have a full-time sustainability manager?
- Detail the key elements of your EMS.

TABLE 10.1 Criteria and Measurements for Supplier Evaluation

Element	Unit of Measure	Current Emission	Initial Baseline	Objective
Direct greenhouse gas emissions (Kyoto)	Metric tons CO_2 or equivalent			
Indirect greenhouse gas emissions (Kyoto)	Metric tons CO_2 or equivalent			
Hazardous waste disposal	Metric tons			
Nonhazardous waste disposal	Metric tons			
Electric energy usage	Giga-joules			
Fuel energy usage	Giga-joules			
Renewable energy use	Giga-joules			
Waste material recycled or reused	Metric tons			

- Please provide a copy of your company's Corporate Social Responsibility policy.
- What is your organization's current carbon footprint, and how are you planning to comply with global warming initiatives?
- Identify any toxic materials used in your processes and how you are controlling them.
- Do you currently generate nonrecyclable waste? Please list.
- Describe your program for reducing waste.
- List your accomplishments and goals for converting to sustainable energy sources.
- What significant amounts of recycled materials do you use in your operations?
- Is your organization currently certified to an environmental standard (such as ISO 14001:2004)? Please list.

If possible, you should also consider the use of hard measurements in your evaluation. Table 10.1 lists some of the criteria and measurements that can be used.

Summary

We began this chapter with some definitions of the term "sustainability" and then outlined some of the important sustainability issues. These relate to the use of materials, toxic discharge, and energy consumption. In the materials section, we described the various methods available for waste reduction, the use of renewable resources and protecting habitats, hazardous materials regulations, and man-made and natural disasters. The section on toxic discharge examined greenhouse gases, carbon footprints, ozone depletion, and pollution. We then described the issues around energy consumption and evolving standards such as renewable portfolio standards.

The next section reviewed currently available standards for sustainability such as ISO 14001, the United Nations Global Compact, and Lean Six Sigma. We concluded with a sustainability outline for supplier evaluation criteria.

CHAPTER 11

Risk

R isk is probably one of the most pervasive topics today in business, sourcing, and supply management. The reason for this is quite logical: The more dependent on suppliers an organization becomes, the more likely that a disruption in supply anywhere along its supply chain can result in the organization's failure to meet its commitments. Supply risk is compounded in operations that conduct a lean approach to resources, where shortages can shut down production, as well as in operations that are environmentally or politically sensitive, where failure can impact an entire nation or geographic area.

In this chapter, we examine the nature of risk in sourcing operations and how organizations are (or should be) dealing with it.

The Nature of Risk

Although definitions of risk are abundant, let's begin our exploration with a definition of our own—in fact, two definitions—that will be useful as we go forward:

1. **Simple definition:** Risk is the chance of something happening that will have an adverse impact on our objectives.
2. **More complex definition:** Risk is a measure of the inability to achieve program objectives within defined cost, schedule, and performance constraints.

In this chapter, we use these two definitions interchangeably. They serve as an anchor point in our illustrations.

Why Is Understanding Risk Important?

Risk affects many aspects of the supply sourcing process; it is a guiding consideration when selecting suppliers. We select those suppliers that are most likely to meet our stated requirements: suppliers with low risk. Risk is also an overriding consideration in ensuring ongoing supplier performance and our continued operation without interruption due to a supplier's failure to meet its commitments.

Uncertainty in the Statement of Work (SOW) we issue with our contract can add to the price of a service through holdbacks or contingency accounts due to vague or complex requirements. This is especially true in construction and research and development projects. And risk can lead to supply interruption or increased cost through contract breach, default, or a supplier's inability to fund its commitments.

We also base many of our key business decisions on the level of risk involved in an action or activity or in the choice of a design solution or a technology. We consider risk as an evaluation factor in choosing between alternative courses of action, often seeking the alternative with the least amount of risk. Thus we typically see risk as a critical aspect of business operations that must be managed properly in order to remain in a tolerable range.

Clearly, effectively monitoring and managing risk is costly when the risk is high and consumes large amounts of critical resources, yet the customer is often blind to the value this produces. As a result, risk management processes must be well understood so that they can be implemented with minimum cost.

Risk Management Principles

With an effective process in place, risk can be managed so that the impact of a potentially catastrophic event can be minimized or avoided altogether. In order to establish this process, you should first be able to recognize and establish several fundamental principles.

When a formal risk management process is first put in place, there is a cultural shift from putting out fires and crisis management within the organization to a much more proactive decision-making method that seeks to avoid problems. Systematically anticipating what events might occur to thwart our objectives becomes a part of everyday business, and the management of risks becomes as integral to supply sourcing as any other process.

What Is Risk Management?

Risk management is the process of identifying, assessing, and controlling risk arising from operational factors and making decisions that balance risk with offsetting benefits (or rewards). It is a systematic approach used to identify, evaluate, and reduce or eliminate the possibility of an unfavorable deviation from an expected outcome.

Risk management is also a process wherein the program or project team is responsible for identifying, analyzing, planning, tracking, controlling, and communicating effectively the risks (and the steps being taken to handle them) within the team's environment. The outcome of this process is communicated to management and stakeholders.

Risk management is also a continuous, iterative process used to manage risk in order to ensure that activities achieve their intended objectives. It should be a key element and an integral part of normal program or project management and engineering planning.

RISK IDENTIFICATION Identifying specific risks is the first step in any risk management process. Let's look at some of the more common categories of risk to consider:

- **Financial risks.** These risks can range from an unexpected and unfavorable change in exchange rates all the way to a supplier's bankruptcy. Some examples of financial risks include budget overruns, funding limitation, unauthorized (constructive) changes, and missed milestones requiring additional funding. Financial risks also encompass unexpected cost overruns that may be linked to other risk factors, such as changes in the scope of work required to successfully complete the activity.
- **Scope or schedule risks.** Largely a result of poor project definition or a poorly worded SOW, these are primarily risks that threaten the timeline but, as noted, can also have cost implications. Schedule changes are often the result of a natural disaster, such as a hurricane, fire, or flood, or due to noncompliance issues generated by a supplier. Scope risk can occur as a result of changes that are required when the initial SOW becomes unworkable or due to technological changes generated by the market.
- **Legal risks.** Legal and contractual risks are often related to disputes or different interpretations of contractual obligations, or from not meeting a requirement included in the terms and conditions. Use or misuse of intellectual property can also be considered a legal risk, especially when patent infringement is a possibility. We can also include in this category violation of laws or regulations and obligations created as a result of changes in the law as well as civil lawsuits.
- **Environmental risk.** In the sourcing process, it is critical to evaluate the risk to the environment created by your supplier or contractor. Environmental risk includes the organization's negative impact on water, air, and soil as a result of discharges, emissions, and other forms of waste.

As noted in Chapter 10, greenhouse gas and ozone-depleting chemicals have become a serious threat to the planet. Industrial waste, too, has to be considered a major concern. Threats to the natural habitat are also coming under very close scrutiny and regulation. Where these factors are present or potentially present, you must monitor them closely; governments worldwide are regulating these conditions to a much greater extent, which may result in significant interruptions should a supplier be affected.

- **Sociopolitical risk.** When the regulatory environment changes in response to a new government or to increasing awareness of inequitable social conditions, many existing institutions experience difficulty in adapting. Sourcing efforts, especially those in low-cost countries, must consider the impact of these changes on the culture and business operations within that environment. Stability comes with a price.
- **Project organization risk.** These risks are generally a result of not having the right people or equipment in the right place at the right time. You might also consider this as a planning risk.
- **Human behavior risks.** Not surprisingly, human behavior risks are the most difficult to assess. Sometimes the project or activity may be placed in jeopardy due to an illness or injury or due to the departure of key personnel; sometimes it may be the result of poor judgment or bad decisions.

> Risk increases with the complexity of any given situation, the number of unknown factors, and the potential consequences of failure.

In addition to the categories just outlined, our assessment should identify if the risks to be considered are internal risks (risks related to our own operations) or external risks (related to conditions outside of our organization, such as market factors, political climate, regulatory environment, economic circumstances, and so on). More specifically:

- **Internal risks** are risks that you can control or influence. Internal risks include cost estimates, staff assignments, schedule delays, and product design.
- **External risks** are risks that you as a contract manager cannot control or influence. External risks include governmental actions relating to taxes that could affect a financial contract, weather delays that could affect a construction contract, and a change in currency rates that could affect the value of an international contract.

A number of techniques and tools may be useful in helping you identify risks. You can adapt these techniques and tools to your current situation:

- **Expert knowledge.** Expert knowledge relies on the experience of people who have worked on similar sourcing operations in the past. Interviews with individuals, stakeholders, and experts are good methods to use to gather expert knowledge. Interviews with subject matter experts may uncover risks not previously considered.
- **Historical information.** You or your colleagues may have compiled a historical database of risks encountered in previous sourcing efforts and contracts. It will be useful if you organized this database by contract type and include a list of the problems encountered that can be identified as risks, their sources, and the events that precipitated them. Also include the mitigation plan put in place to deal with the risk and the success of that mitigation plan if it was actually applied to an event. Records of previous contracts can also provide historical information. These records may be kept in a database, or they may be paper files. If you don't currently have a process that captures historical risk information, you should consider developing one.
- **Brainstorming.** Another technique frequently noted is to identify risks and sources of risk by conducting a brainstorming session. Gather a group of subject matter experts who have an understanding of the nature of risk; include stakeholders as well as those who will not be directly affected by your activities as a way of maintaining relative objectivity. This activity will make it possible to create a broad list of potential risk events and their sources. You can then apply them to your specific conditions in order to refine the list.

  A variation of brainstorming often used is called the Delphi method, a means of leveraging the collective judgment of specialists and/or management (often referred to as "expert judgment"). We use this process primarily when objective and quantitative data for measurement and decision making do not exist (or possibly even make sense). You can use this technique to determine outcomes such as how long it might take to draft a contract, what penalty limits you should set, or how long negotiations may last. This technique consists of three simple steps:

1. Ask participants to estimate a value for some occurrence, usually anonymously on paper.
2. Consolidate results, and ask participants with responses outside the norm to justify their positions for each participant's benefit and/or reconsideration. Ask all participants to estimate the value of the occurrence.

3. Consolidate the results from Step 2, and repeat the process until you reach a reasonably close value.

- **Simulations.** Several analysis tools are commonly available for providing simulations. One that is frequently used is the Monte Carlo simulation. Monte Carlo simulation provides the user with a range of possible outcomes and the probabilities they will occur for any choice of action. A number of software products can help develop models; several of them work with MS Excel. The decision tree diagram is also a useful simulation tool that can depict key interactions among decisions and associated chance events.
- **Checklists.** Through research, you may be able to develop a useful checklist to run through whenever needed during sourcing activities. You can use historical data that applies to similar activities in your organization or find related information through a well-directed Web search.

As you conduct your sourcing activities, you can go over this list to determine if any apply to current activities and if the sources being considered pose potential risks for this contract. Although checklists can be useful tools, they should not replace close analysis of the conditions you might encounter. It is also unlikely that even the most detailed checklist will include every potential risk in a particular situation.

RISK ASSESSMENT   Risks such as the ones mentioned are closely related to the circumstances of the project or activity, and their implications vary widely from situation to situation. Consequently, it is incumbent on sourcing personnel to review the specific situation in terms of the risk categories noted earlier in order to define the risks that may apply in any given case. This is the first step in the assessment process, but it can also be the most complex since many of the situations we must work with are fluid and ever changing. When we add in the many variable factors in most sourcing plans, we find that an assessment of risk is often simply a matter of guesswork, since what we can observe lacks any discernible pattern.

Probably the best we can do is to keep our assessments simple. Once we have identified the elements of potential risk, we will need a very simple method of evaluating or measuring them to determine which require our attention, now and in the future. In simplifying our assessment, we generally have to ignore the interaction of individual elements with one another and opt for examining the elements in isolation, for the most part. It would be virtually impossible given the common tools we have available to try to examine, for example, the impact that a supplier's decision to take on additional work beyond its capacity would have on its ability to commit funds to our project. So we are forced to look at each risk—exceeding capacity and committing funds—separately.

A very simple method in common practice can be used to examine these risks. We examine each element of risk in terms of its likelihood of occurrence (the probability that a program or project will experience an undesired event) and its impact (the consequences or severity of the undesired event, should it actually occur). Some examples of an undesired event include a cost overrun, schedule slippage, safety mishap, health problem, malicious activities, environmental impact, or failure to achieve a needed scientific or technological breakthrough.

A brainstorming-based risk assessment facilitated session with stakeholders, team members, and infrastructure support staff is the most common technique used to identify risks and evaluate their potentials. The primary source of information is historical data developed from activities similar to the one we are evaluating, with an added element of human judgment and intuition. This form of facilitated session is also known as force-field analysis. By using qualitative terms such as *very high, high, moderate, low*, and *very low* to identify the probability of risk occurring, you can prioritize the risks associated with sourcing and with the contract that follows, then map the analysis to specific phases of the contract, specific business units, parties to a contract, and so on.

Once we have identified individual risk characteristics, we can assign some relative criteria to each of the categories. Along with the descriptions, we will include a relative measure. Table 11.1 is an example of what that might look like, beginning with descriptions of each probability and consequence.

TABLE 11.1 Risk Assessment with Probable Outcomes

Probability		Consequence	
Rating	Description	Rating	Description
Almost certain (.90)	Will occur in most instances	Catastrophic (.90)	Project cancellation
Likely (.70)	Could occur in most instances	Major (.70)	Significant time or cost overruns
Moderate (.50)	Should occur at some time	Moderate (.50)	Some time or cost overruns
Unlikely (.30)	Might occur occasionally	Minor (.30)	Some inconvenience
Rare (.10)	Will occur only in exceptional circumstances	Insignificant (.10)	Little noticeable effect

TABLE 11.2 Calculated Risk Assessment

Risk	Description	Probability	Consequence	Score
Design	Fails to work effectively	.60	.90	.54
Key personnel	Lead engineer leaves	.40	.50	.20
Ramp up	Late delivery of equipment	.50	.50	.25
Production	Lower yield than expected	.40	.40	.16
Sales	Not marketable at price	.20	.40	.08

The criteria and scale shown in Table 11.2 are an example of a calculated risk assessment. Very simply, we multiply the probability factor by the consequence factor. As you can see, at the time of this particular assessment, the risk of design failure is the most significant. In fact, we would likely consider any score above .35 as sufficient to require ongoing tracking. For this particular situation, sourcing activities based on design criteria would be a bit premature, although some market analysis would still be in order as a means of gaining a head start should the current design be released. Keep in mind, though, that as time progresses, additional criteria may surface, and the ratings shown may change.

Risk Control

Every contract is written around a product or service. The nature of that product or service has a major effect on the risks identified. If the product has been provided successfully many times in the past, there will be fewer unidentified risks, and you will have a history of dealing with them.

After identifying and categorizing the risks, you must take steps to control them. The notion of control acknowledges that you may not be able to *eliminate* risk entirely in many situations.

Instead, you may be able to minimize the risk or mitigate it by taking action to handle the unwanted outcome in an acceptable way. Options may also be available that will enable you to avoid the risk altogether or transfer the risk to your supplier, when beneficial to both parties.

The approach or tool you use for control will largely depend on the stage in the contract where the risk appears and on the amount of information available regarding the source or impact of that risk. Regardless of the conditions, however, effective control requires a plan or at the very least an outline of actions we should be taking and the circumstances under which we should take them.

As you develop a plan, you must take into account the goal, scope, and objectives of the sourcing activity. You must clearly understand the product or service being provided, its purpose, and the expectations of the customer or stakeholders regarding the product. You also need to understand how the contract and its product support your organization's strategic goals and business plans. This knowledge will help you prioritize your activities.

Some of the key elements of a risk control plan will likely consist of one or more of the concepts discussed next.

RISK TRIGGERS A risk trigger can be defined as a precursor to an actual risk event. It lets you know a risk event may be about to occur. You should identify triggers for each significant risk, and you should monitor those triggers, being alert to their appearance as you manage a sourcing operation or contract.

For example, cost overruns on early activities may be a signal that cost estimates were poorly developed and the contract is trending toward being over budget. The person responsible for monitoring the risk would be tracking the costs on those early activities. Cost overruns by a specified date would indicate that cost estimates should be reevaluated.

Another example: A vendor missing a scheduled ship date may be a signal that hardware will not be delivered on time to meet the contracted date. The risk monitor would be responsible for checking with the vendor to make sure items were shipped on the specified date.

MONITORING Monitoring includes tracking current conditions through reports or through physical access to the source. It also includes updated assessments of probability and consequences as well as uncovering conditions that were not apparent previously.

You monitor risks to ensure that:

- Risk responses have been implemented as planned.
- Risk responses are as effective as you expected them to be. If they're not you may have to develop new responses.
- Any documented assumptions remain valid.
- Risk exposure has not changed from its prior state. If it has changed, additional analysis is needed.
- No risk trigger has occurred. If a trigger has occurred, contingency plans must be put in place.
- Proper policies and procedures are followed.
- No risks have occurred that were not previously identified. Again, if new risks have arisen, they must go through the same review and analysis process as previously identified risks.

MITIGATION Risk mitigation involves lessening the impact or magnitude of a risk event. You can do this by reducing the probability that the risk will occur, reducing the risk event's impact, or both, to an acceptable level. One way to reduce the probability of a risk occurring is by using proven technology to lessen the chances that the product of the contract will not work. If the contracted service is a software application, you could elect to develop on a platform that you've used successfully in the past rather than on a platform with which you have little or no experience. Purchasing insurance to protect against weather damage on a construction project is a way to mitigate the financial impact of a risk event related to bad weather.

As you mitigate risks, you may end up trading one risk for another. For example, a buyer may choose to mitigate a cost risk by asking for a fixed price contract, but that may cause a schedule risk if the contractor is not able to provide the service in the desired time frame for the fixed price.

Costs for risk mitigation should be in line with the probability and consequences of the risk. In other words, you'll spend less time and money planning for risks with low probability and low impact than for risks with high probability and/or high impact. To aid decision making about risk reduction, you must take into account the cost of reducing the risk. We call "risk leverage" the difference in risk exposure divided by the cost of reducing the risk. In other words, risk reduction leverage is:

$$\frac{(\text{Risk exposure before reduction}) - (\text{Risk exposure after reduction})}{(\text{Cost of risk reduction})}$$

CONTINGENCY PLANS   A common method of mitigating the impact of a risk event is to develop a contingency plan in advance of the possible occurrence, usually shortly after the risk is identified. The purpose of the contingency plan is to enable the sustained execution of mission-critical processes and information technology systems in the event of an extraordinary event that causes these systems to fail to meet minimum requirements. The contingency plan will assess the needs and requirements so that your organization may be prepared to respond to the event in order to regain operation of the systems made inoperable by the event.

The plan includes specific actions to be taken should a risk event occur, such as identifying an alternate source if the selected source becomes unable to meet its contractual obligations, or a substitute part if the primary part becomes unavailable.

AVOIDANCE   If you can identify the specific cause of a risk, it is more likely that you will be able to reduce or eliminate it. For example, if the lack of skilled resources causes an identified risk, you can eliminate the risk by having the supplier hire the skills needed to perform the contracted services. Risk avoidance techniques also include reducing the scope of the contract to avoid high-risk elements, adding resources or time to the contract, avoiding suppliers or contractors with unproven track records, and using a proven approach instead of a new one.

ACCEPTANCE   You may choose to accept the consequences of the risk event. Risk assumption can be active, as in developing a contingency plan for execution should the risk event occur, or passive, as in deciding to deal with the risks and their consequences when or if they occur but not planning for them in advance.

TRANSFER   Transferring the risk occurs by allocating risks to other entities or by buying insurance to cover any financial loss, should the risk become a reality. In some situations, your supplier may be better suited to dealing with a particular risk, so transferring it through negotiations might be in order. There is a caveat, however: Risk transfer may come with additional cost, such as the cost of insurance or an additional amount tacked on to the pricing by the supplier in order to deal with the event should it occur.

Summary

This chapter is by no means an exhaustive study of risk in sourcing operations, but we trust we have touched on the key points so that you can understand the nature of risk and its associated elements.

We began this chapter with some definitions and an explanation of the nature of risk, covering why an understanding of risk is important. Examining risk management principles, we categorized risks as related to financial, scope or schedule, legal, environmental, sociopolitical project organization, and human behavior factors; we also pointed out the difference between internal and external risk factors.

From there we turned our attention to tools that can be useful in identifying risks, such as leveraging expert knowledge and historical information, brainstorming and using the Delphi technique, and the use of simulations and checklists. Following this, we examined risk assessment and simple methods used to evaluate risk, such as using the probability/consequence matrix to identify the level of risk we may be facing.

Looking at risk control, we pointed out the importance of planning. We then covered the elements of risk control, such as identifying risk triggers, monitoring risk, mitigating risk, and developing contingency plans. Finally, we noted the characteristics of risk avoidance, risk acceptance, and risk transfer.

CHAPTER 12

Global Sourcing

Over the past decade, the emergence of China as the United States' major supplier of manufactured goods has underscored what we have known for some time: The world is rapidly becoming a single marketplace. As the cost of labor and capital equipment increases in developed nations, manufacturers naturally turn to low-cost country producers. Not only can these countries provide lower labor rates, but often their newer facilities are much more advanced and productive than counterparts in developed countries, largely due to the more recent capital investments of multinational corporations.

The movement toward significantly increased international trade has been facilitated by a number of other key factors: improved communication tools, readily available transportation, automated Customs processing, lower labor rates coupled with a technically proficient and well-educated workforce, to mention a few. In addition to manufactured goods, these conditions also enable the outsourcing of traditional U.S. services, such as programming, call centers, and engineering to offshore locations. Outsourcing, by definition, is the transfer of a function traditionally performed internally by an organization to an external supplier. Outsourcing to offshore nations, then, provides the major impetus for international sourcing as a discipline.

Although the most prevalent reason cited for global sourcing is to lower costs, there is also significant advantage in developing a broader supply base, increasing the number of possible suppliers from which the buying firm can select. Increased competition will typically enable lower costs and provide competitive pressure to suppliers that usually results in increased overall value. Overseas sources in some industries are more advanced technologically than existing U.S. counterparts and can provide greater productivity because of newer capital equipment. Many have unused capacity, which can be an attractive asset to companies that have maxed out current capacity. Broadening the supply base internationally, however, does not mean increasing the number of suppliers. It means increasing the opportunity to find *better* suppliers, thereby enabling the buying firm to decrease the number of contracted suppliers and pursue collaborative or alliance relationships when appropriate.

We examine these factors and other related aspects of global sourcing in the coming sections.

Developing a Global Sourcing Strategy

Companies that engage or intend to engage in international procurement need to develop a global sourcing strategy and incorporate it into their strategic plan. The strategy should include a set of criteria for making decisions to use international sources, the methods to be used in sourcing (such as using intermediaries), contract formation requirements, and a plan for continued monitoring of performance—essentially, most of the important elements in any sourcing strategy. The complexity lies in the cultural differences, the risks, and the extended logistical requirements encountered in global trade. These need to be accounted for in a global sourcing strategy.

Strategic Plan Elements

There is likely no need to develop a separate strategic plan for expanding sourcing operations to foreign countries, but there may be some aspects that have not been specifically included and should be considered. What is most important is to review your organization's objectives to ensure that your overseas activities will be in alignment with them. Some key objectives, other than reduced cost, might include access to new skills and technology, access to additional capacity, increased competition, and the opportunity to revamp existing processes. You may also have to address the impact of potentially longer lead times and additional transportation costs. If any of these apply and are not already included in your strategic sourcing plan, they should be developed and added. (See Chapter 1 for a refresher on strategic planning.)

MARKET ANALYSIS   Market analysis has a significant role in creating a global sourcing strategy. Beginning with an internal analysis of categories that show the likelihood of reduced cost through offshore sourcing, along with a complete spending profile for that category, the analysis should include and examine these aspects:

- Identify key global suppliers, their markets, and where their major customers are located. Understand if and how they compete with one another.

- Match your company's requirements to the capabilities of those suppliers to determine if there is a potential fit in terms of technology and capacity.
- Analyze suppliers' financial positions, both long term and short term. Gathering data may be difficult, and it may be necessary to engage a third party with expertise in that market segment.
- Examine market trends in those areas to provide a comparison with current sources of supply. Be sure to look at economic levers, political stability, and product development trends to ensure that they are in alignment with your company's forecasted requirements.
- Determine if cost profiles provide an opportunity for savings.
- Ensure detailed specifications exist for the products you are considering transferring.
- Are materials required for production available locally? Are substitutions possible?
- Establish transportation requirements to determine if they can be met.
- Identify areas of risk and uncertainty, understanding how they can be effectively controlled.

LOW-COST COUNTRY SOURCING   Companies have been able to realize significant savings, reportedly up to 40 percent, in countries that are identified as low cost. Typically, these countries are in emerging regions where there may be some offsetting risk as supply chains are developed. Countries currently classified as low-cost producers include:

- Brazil
- Bulgaria
- China
- India
- Philippines
- Romania
- Thailand
- Ukraine
- Vietnam

INTERNATIONAL PROCUREMENT SERVICES   Many expert sourcing and supply management services can be found in most areas where companies in developed nations are currently trading. These services can provide some significant advantages, as long as the additional cost is in line with potential savings. They can be used to provide a skilled and effective local sourcing team that has access to the necessary resources for supplier qualification, quality management, logistics management, and engineering and design support. These firms can also assist with communication and help to create strong, sustainable relationships with contracted suppliers. And, importantly, they can be used to establish a "home office" facility to support staff travel to suppliers in their region.

For casual or occasional overseas purchases, your sourcing team may want to simply use an online sourcing directory. Several exist that provide both source identification and source qualification data, similar to information that could be gathered through a Request for Information. One source that we have found useful is Alibaba (www.alibaba.com). One of the largest online catalog aggregators and sourcing sites, Alibaba provides information on products and services across the alphabet. Although the company is based in China, the site provides information in all countries engaged in international trade.

These sites provide very similar services, although some are locally or regionally focused:

- **B2Brazil** (www.b2brazil.com/B2Brazil/principal)
- **B2B Manufacturers** (www.manufacturers.com.tw)
- **China.cn** (http://en.china.cn)
- **DIY Trade** (www.diytrade.com)
- **EC21** (www.ec21.com)
- **ECVV** (www.ecvv.com)
- **Global Sources** (www.globalsources.com)
- **Hong Kong Trade Development Center** (www.hktdc.com)
- **Ketera** (www.ketera.com)
- **Trade India** (www.tradeindia.com)
- **Trade Key** (www.tradekey.com)

Additional Criteria for International Sourcing

As part of operational planning and prior to engaging in offshore sourcing, it is important to understand and incorporate those general supplier selection criteria that supplement your standard selection criteria. To help you do so, we have outlined a number of requirements that generally apply to international sourcing for you to consider:

- **Market analysis.** Market analysis is considerably more complex when potential sources are spread over several nations. Data, especially financial data, are often very difficult to come by, so you may be forced to rely on consultants or external sourcing experts to help identify suitable suppliers and local business trends. Key questions to answer: Does the supplier have the expertise needed, the financial capability to perform, and the ability to ramp up production if needed?

- **Skills.** Levels of training vary widely from country to country. You will want to understand how the potential suppliers' employees are trained and qualified and at what competency level they operate compared to your current supplier.
- **Key personnel.** Try to find out the turnover rate of key personnel. Are they experienced or new to the industry or industry segment?
- **Culture and language.** Will you be able to understand one another, and can cultural differences be overcome? (Refer back to Chapters 4 and 8 for more details.) Keep in mind, too, that quality concepts also differ in other cultures.
- **Contracting and legal systems.** You will be working with a variety of legal systems in which U.S. contract terms may not be understood or accepted. You will need to consider how you will deal with this variation and enforce the terms of your contracts.
- **Logistics.** You will want to check out available shipping methods and costs, along with the cost of export and import tariffs.
- **Currency.** When you consider the financial risks of global sourcing, you must choose the best currency for pricing in order to minimize currency fluctuation risk. If you price in the supplier's currency, the supplier is relieved of currency risk. Floating currency strategy (where the currency value can vary with market conditions) performs well with market-driven products. Pegged currency (one whose value is tied to another currency or currencies) can be used with a cost-driven product. Countries with pegged currencies are generally smaller ones, such as Taiwan, Thailand, Hong Kong, and Korea.

  Hedging is a strategy that protects the dollar value of a future foreign currency cash flow. The buyer avoids the risk of adverse currency fluctuations by using forward or futures contracts or via currency options.
- **Payment terms.** The selling firm usually requests Letters of Credit. Such a letter is an instrument issued by a bank that promises to pay a specific amount of money upon presentation of required documents—generally proof of correct shipment. An open billing account settled by wire transfer is becoming increasingly common and can provide the same terms as those provided domestically.
- **Communication.** Beyond the language barrier, you need to assess the frequency of personal contact required and the time differences.
- **Risks.** For obvious reasons, including the criteria listed, risk can increase significantly with offshore sources. Risks are outlined in Chapter 11, but you may want to place extra emphasis on political and economic stability if you intend to engage in long-term operations. You also should understand the natural risks in the area: earthquakes, hurricanes, and so on.

- **References.** Check local and international references regarding past performance and problems encountered and any official government blacklist designating terrorist organizations.
- **Intellectual property.** Many cultures do not place the same emphasis on protecting intellectual property as we do. For example, many in China view intellectual property as a form of exploitation by Western countries; as a result, they believe they have a right to that property. Our concept of private property is relatively new and even unknown in some countries. This is an important consideration for many companies engaged in offshore sourcing. If it is of concern, you will need to conduct additional research into the practices and laws of the particular country you intend to do business in and perhaps consult with local legal experts.

Source Selection

After allowing for additional transportation costs (and time), source selection processes for international suppliers should be little different from domestic source selection. Virtually all of the same criteria apply. There are, however, some tools provided by the World Trade Organization (www.wto.org), the World Bank (www.worldbank.org), the United Nations Commodity Trade Database (http://comtrade.un.org), and the U.S. International Trade Administration (http://trade.gov). In addition, most countries have trade facility web sites (including the U.S. Department of Commerce) that can provide information on the types of businesses in their locations capable of conducting international trade.

Statistics

Where does your research begin? Likely, you will want to look at existing trade locations. A number of statistics drawn from various sources that may be good information to help you get started are presented in the next tables.

Table 12.1 shows a relatively current listing of U.S. import volumes based on country. The difference between years 2008 and 2009 clearly reflects the economics of the period.

Some additional information available from the World Bank and the United Nations provides demographic information that may be useful. Table 12.2 shows a particularly useful report from the United Nations.

International Trade Requirements

Overseas sourcing typically requires attention to a number of regulatory requirements and legal aspects of trade that often differ from domestic

TABLE 12.1 Imports from Major U.S. Trading Partners (Listed by 2009 Trade Volume)

Partner	2008	2009
World	2,103,640,710,944	1,559,624,813,477
China	337,772,627,823	296,373,883,488
Canada	339,491,425,363	226,248,448,986
Mexico	215,941,618,934	176,654,372,581
Japan	139,262,197,032	95,803,683,368
Germany	97,496,573,724	71,498,154,314
United Kingdom	58,587,383,031	47,479,890,559
South Korea	48,069,078,711	39,215,588,565
France	44,049,335,702	34,236,042,957
Taiwan	36,326,075,377	28,362,148,998
Ireland	31,346,482,641	28,100,577,524
Venezuela	51,423,628,380	28,059,033,911
Italy	36,134,975,141	26,429,788,240
Malaysia	30,736,075,258	23,282,618,764
Saudi Arabia	54,747,448,525	22,053,149,818
India	25,704,382,575	21,165,965,968
Brazil	30,452,944,177	20,069,606,594
Nigeria	38,068,007,014	19,128,179,390
Thailand	23,538,275,396	19,082,487,689
Israel	22,335,834,788	18,744,356,591
Russian Federation	26,782,985,455	18,199,650,572

procedures. Beyond the obvious—that laws and regulations vary by country—there are import and export restrictions that must be observed. Many countries levy tariffs on both imports and exports, and virtually all require export inspections by Customs officials. Understanding these requirements must be placed very high on your sourcing checklist to ensure that cost savings do not vanish as a result of unanticipated expenses.

Legal Aspects of International Trade

Since the Uniform Commercial Code (UCC) does not apply outside of the U.S., the terms and conditions on U.S. purchase orders will not provide much protection. However, many countries have agreed to abide by the United Nations Convention on Contracts for the International Sale of Goods, known commonly as CISG, which provides standardized terms in much the same way as does the UCC. You should spend some time reviewing this document, which you can access at www.cisg.law.pace.edu/cisg/text/treaty.html.

Several important U.S. regulations control international trade to one extent or another. Those that you should be particularly aware of include:

TABLE 12.2 Human Development Index: Derived from Indices of Life Expectancy, Education, and Gross Domestic Product

Very High Human Development	High Human Development
1. Norway	39. Bahrain
2. Australia	40. Estonia
3. Iceland	41. Poland
4. Canada	42. Slovakia
5. Ireland	43. Hungary
6. Netherlands	44. Chile
7. Sweden	45. Croatia
8. France	46. Lithuania
9. Switzerland	47. Antigua and Barbuda
10. Japan	48. Latvia
11. Luxembourg	49. Argentina
12. Finland	50. Uruguay
13. United States	51. Cuba
14. Austria	52. Bahamas
15. Spain	53. Mexico
16. Denmark	54. Costa Rica
17. Belgium	55. Libyan Arab Jamahiriya
18. Italy	56. Oman
19. Liechtenstein	57. Seychelles
20. New Zealand	58. Venezuela (Bolivarian Republic of)
21. United Kingdom	59. Saudi Arabia
22. Germany	60. Panama
23. Singapore	61. Bulgaria
24. Hong Kong, China (SAR)	62. Saint Kitts and Nevis
25. Greece	63. Romania
26. Korea (Republic of)	64. Trinidad and Tobago
27. Israel	65. Montenegro
28. Andorra	66. Malaysia
29. Slovenia	67. Serbia
30. Brunei Darussalam	68. Belarus
31. Kuwait	69. Saint Lucia
32. Cyprus	70. Albania
33. Qatar	71. Russian Federation
34. Portugal	72. The former Yugoslav Republic of Macedonia
35. United Arab Emirates	73. Dominica
36. Czech Republic	74. Grenada
37. Barbados	75. Brazil
38. Malta	76. Bosnia and Herzegovina
	77. Colombia
	78. Peru
	79. Turkey
	80. Ecuador
	81. Mauritius
	82. Kazakhstan
	83. Lebanon

Source: United Nations Development Programme, *Human Development Report 2009*, HDI Rankings, http://hdr.undp.org/en/statistics.

- **Foreign Corrupt Practices Act.** The Foreign Corrupt Practices Act of 1977 (FCPA) is federal law that:

   prohibits U.S. companies and citizens, foreign companies listed on a U.S. stock exchange, or any person acting while in the United States, from corruptly paying or offering to pay, directly or indirectly, money or anything of value to a foreign official to obtain or retain business (the "Anti-bribery Provisions"). The FCPA also requires "issuers" (any company including foreign companies with securities traded on a U.S. exchange or otherwise required to file periodic reports with the Securities and Exchange Commission ("SEC")) to keep books and records that accurately reflect business transactions and to maintain effective internal controls (the "Books and Records and Internal Control Provisions").

   The FCPA is jointly enforced by the Department of Justice ("DOJ") and the SEC. Proof of a U.S. territorial nexus is not required for the FCPA to be implicated against U.S. companies and citizens, and FCPA violations can, and often do, occur even if the prohibited activity takes place entirely outside of the United States. For this reason, business leaders must be knowledgeable about all business activity, including activity that takes place thousands of miles away from corporate headquarters.

   For the full text, visit www.justice.gov/criminal/fraud/fcpa/statutes/regulations.html.
- **International Traffic in Arms Regulation (ITAR).** This U.S. law controls the export and import of military- and national security–related articles and services, administered by the Directorate of Defense Trade Controls of the U.S. State Department. ITAR requirements change periodically so it is important to review the listing before engaging in activities that may be controlled. You can get more information at this web site: www.pmddtc.state.gov/regulations_laws/itar_official.html
- **Trafficking Victims Protection Reauthorization Act of 2008— Title I: Combating International Trafficking in Persons.** This act was passed by Congress to help prevent trafficking, forced labor, enticement into slavery, sex trafficking of children, and sex tourism by U.S. citizens both in the United States and in foreign countries. Essentially, the act makes it a federal crime punishable by up to 20 years in prison for engaging in the cited activities and having knowledge of these activities without reporting them. This also applies to U.S. contracting firms whose overseas subcontractors engage in such activities.

Import Operations

There are a number of formal considerations and requirements to be aware of when engaged in international trade. While many of these are related to the transportation of goods, you should become familiar with a number of areas before taking up sourcing activities. Some highlights of those you may encounter most frequently are presented next.

TARIFFS   Tariffs are duties (or taxes) applied to goods transported from one country to another, or on imported products. Tariffs raise the prices of imported goods, thus making them less competitive within the market of the importing country.

The Harmonized Tariff System (HTS) is an international commodity classification system, developed under the auspices of Customs Cooperation Council and adopted by the United States in 1989. The HTS assigns a number to each product that is traded internationally to ensure that Customs officers and statisticians around the world are referring to the same thing when classifying a product. It is increasingly the most widely accepted import/export classification methodology and replaces Schedule B export codes and Tariff Schedule of the U.S. import codes. Almost all countries now use the HTS.

Each country can assign on its own four additional numbers, making the entire number 10 digits. The United States does this with its Schedule B system, which is used to describe exports from the United States. Many countries, though, do not use 10 digits; some use only 6 or 8.

Tariffs may be levied in two basic ways: specific tariffs and ad valorem tariffs. An ad valorem tariff is levied as a fixed percentage of the value of the commodity imported. *Ad valorem* is Latin for "on value" or "in proportion to the value." The United States currently levies a 2.5 percent ad valorem tariff on imported automobiles. Thus, if $100,000 worth of autos are imported, the U.S. government collects $2,500 in tariff revenue. In this case, $2,500 is collected whether two $50,000 BMWs are imported or ten $10,000 Hyundais.

A specific tariff is levied as a fixed charge per unit of imports. For example, the U.S. government levies a $0.51 specific tariff on every wristwatch imported into the United States. Thus, if 1,000 watches are imported, the U.S. government collects $510 in tariff revenue. In this case, $510 is collected whether the watch is a $40 Swatch or a $5,000 Rolex.

Occasionally both a specific and an ad valorem tariff are levied on the same product simultaneously. This is known as a two-part tariff. For example, wristwatches imported into the United States face the $0.51 specific tariff as well as a 6.25 percent ad valorem tariff on the case and the strap and a 5.3 percent ad valorem tariff on the battery. Perhaps this should be called a three-part tariff!

CUSTOMS   Customs is both the agency and the process controlling and taxing imports and exports for nations. Today, two automated tools characterize these systems. Customs uses the HTS to control tariff rates on imports.

The Automated Broker Interface (ABI) is the part of the Customs Automated Commercial System that allows participants to file import data with Customs electronically. ABI features include filing and clearing of import freight, payment of Customs duties, querying of quota and tariff status, and interface with other government agencies. This program is available to brokers, importers, carriers, port authorities, and independent service centers. Currently over 96 percent of all entries filed with Customs are filed electronically via the ABI system. You can find relevant codes (known as Section B) at this web site: www.census.gov/foreign-trade/schedules/b.

TRANSPORTATION   You should become familiar with three key transportation roles:

1. **Freight forwarders** combine small shipments from different shippers into larger shipments for scale economies in the purchase of intercity transportation. Freight forwarders function as wholesalers of transportation services—specialists in traffic operations, Customs clearances and shipping, and tariffs and schedules. They assist exporters in determining and paying freight, fees, and insurance charges. They usually handle freight from port of export to overseas port of import. In the United States, they are licensed by the Federal Maritime Commission.
2. **Customs brokers** are people or firms licensed by an importer's government and engaged in entering and clearing goods through Customs. Brokers' responsibilities include preparing the entry form and filing it; advising the importer on duties to be paid; advancing duties and other costs; and arranging for delivery to the importer.
3. **Logistics providers** are known by the terms "3PL" or "4PL," referring to third-party or fourth-party logistics providers, a means of describing the level of services offered. Logistics providers were introduced into the supply chain to convey that deep informational technology skills and deeper analytical skills were required to achieve supply chain leadership. But the term "4PL" is better defined in context of the global marketplace, where outsourcing logistics creates more than a supplier/customer relationship: It creates a partnership that is critical to the success of the venture.

TRANSPORTATION TERMS (INCOTERMS)   INCOTERMS 2000 are internationally accepted commercial terms defining the respective roles of the buyer and seller in the arrangement of transportation and other responsibilities. They also clarify when the transfer of ownership of the merchandise takes place.

INCOTERMS are used in conjunction with a sales agreement or other method of transacting the sale and replace commonly used U.S. terms in international shipments.

Here is a brief summary of the terms and their meanings:

- **EXW—Ex Works.** Title and risk pass to the buyer. Includes payment of all transportation and insurance costs. Used for any mode of transportation.
- **FCA—Free Carrier.** Title and risk pass to the buyer when the seller delivers goods cleared for export to the carrier. The seller must load goods on the buyer's vehicle. The buyer is obligated to receive the seller's arriving vehicle unloaded.
- **FAS—Free Alongside Ship.** Title and risk pass to the buyer once delivered alongside the ship by the seller.
- **FOB—Free On Board.** Title and risk pass to the buyer, including payment of all transportation and insurance costs once delivered on board the ship by the seller. Used for sea or inland waterway transportation.
- **CFR—Cost and Freight.** Title, risk, and insurance costs pass to the buyer when delivered on board the ship by the seller, who pays the transportation cost to the destination port. Used for sea or inland waterway transportation.
- **CIF—Cost, Insurance, and Freight.** Title and risk pass to the buyer when delivered on board the ship by the seller, who pays transportation and insurance costs to destination port. Used for sea or inland waterway transportation.
- **CPT—Carriage Paid To.** Title, risk, and insurance costs pass to the buyer when delivered to the carrier by the seller, who pays transportation costs to destination. Used for any mode of transportation.
- **CIP—Carriage and Insurance Paid To.** Title and risk pass to the buyer when delivered to the carrier by the seller, who pays transportation and insurance costs to destination. Used for any mode of transportation.
- **DAF—Delivered at Frontier.** Title, risk, and responsibility for import clearance pass to the buyer when delivered to a named border point by the seller. Used for any mode of transportation.
- **DES—Delivered Ex Ship.** Title, risk, and responsibility for vessel discharge and import clearance pass to the buyer when the seller delivers goods on board the ship to destination port. Used for sea or inland waterway transportation.
- **DEQ—Delivered Ex Quay (Duty Paid).** Title and risk pass to the buyer when delivered on board the ship at the destination point by the seller, who delivers goods on dock at destination point cleared for import. Used for sea or inland waterway transportation.

- **DDU—Delivered Duty Unpaid.** The seller fulfills his or her obligation when goods have been made available at the named place in the country of importation.
- **DDP—Delivered Duty Paid.** Title and risk pass to the buyer when the seller delivers goods to a named destination point cleared for import. Used for any mode of transportation.

Generally, buyers prefer to use CIF or DDP as the terms providing the lowest cost. EXW, CPT, CIP, DAF, DDU, and DDP are commonly used for any mode of transportation; FAS, FOB, CFR, CIF, DES, and DEQ are used for sea and inland waterway transportation.

DOCUMENTATION Moving goods from one country to another generally requires the use of documents such as the Bill of Lading (B/L). This is the document issued on behalf of the carrier describing the kind and quantity of goods being shipped, the shipper, the consignee, the ports of loading and discharge, and the carrying vessel. It serves as a document of title, a contract of carriage, and a receipt of goods. If it is a straight B/L, the foreign buyer can obtain the shipment from the carrier simply by showing proof of identity. If a negotiable B/L is used, the buyer must first pay for the goods, post the bond, or meet other conditions agreeable to the seller.

In addition to the standard B/L, a number of other documents may exist to cover the movement of goods. These generally include variations on the standard B/L, such as the House Airway (or Ocean) Bill of Lading or a Master Airway (or Ocean) Bill of Lading.

In addition, import documentation requirements include a Certificate of Origin. This is a document required by Customs that certifies the country of origin of the merchandise.

Summary

This chapter outlined the key elements of global sourcing, beginning with a section on developing a global sourcing strategy and including it in the strategic plan. Integral to the plan are elements such as market analysis, sourcing by country (low cost), using international procurement services, and online sourcing. We also provided an outline of some additional criteria for international sourcing, including skill levels, key personnel, culture and language, contracting and legal systems, logistics, currency considerations, payment terms, communication, risks, reference checking, and some concerns related to intellectual property.

Then we moved on to source selection considerations, providing some statistics and sources of data, along with a list of the major countries from which the United States imports. We also provided a listing of countries in the upper echelons of the Human Development Index provided by the United Nations Development Programme.

In the last section of the chapter, we provided an overview of international trade requirements covering legal aspects of foreign trade, such as the FCPA and ITAR. The chapter concluded with an examination of import operations including tariffs, Customs, transportation considerations, INCOTERMS, and basic documentation requirements.

Glossary

Acceptance testing Testing performed to determine whether a product meets the requirements specified in the contract or by the user and whether to accept it or not.

Accounts Payable Money an organization owes to suppliers for products and services purchased on credit. Also refers to the internal department that processes such payments.

Acquisition Acquisition occurs on a number of levels. In procurement, it refers to the purchase (and, sometimes, sourcing) of a particular product or service.

Alliance A formal but not legally binding relationship between two organizations; in the supply management field, it generally refers to a buyer/seller relationship. Alliances and partnerships can provide strategic advantages in the sales and acquisition of goods and services.

Authority A specific right granted by a principal to an agent to act on its behalf and enter into legally binding actions. See also *Agency*.

Agency Delegated authority to act on behalf of an employer as an agent.

Best value According to the U.S. Federal Acquisition Regulations (FAR), best value means "the expected outcome of an acquisition that, in the Government's estimation, provides the greatest overall benefit in response to the requirement."

Another federal agency (The Department of Transportation, Federal Highway Administration, www.fhwa.dot.gov/reports/designbuild/designbuilda1.htm) describes it this way:

The overall maximum value of the proposal to a sponsor after considering all of the evaluation factors described in the specifications for the project including but not limited to the time needed for performance of the contract, innovative design approaches, the scope and quality of the work, work management, aesthetics, project control, and total project cost of the formulas or other criteria for establishing the parameters for the Best Value are generally clearly defined with the goal of being objective.

Business ethics Adherence to a moral and legal Code of Conduct that defines right and wrong in a business context.

Business Process Outsourcing (BPO) The outsourcing to a third party of various types of business functions and processes such as procurement, accounting, human resources, and logistics.

Carbon footprint A measure of the amount of carbon dioxide emitted into the atmosphere; a measure of the greenhouse gases that are produced by activities of a person, a family, a school, or a business that involve burning fossil fuels.

Category A specific commodity or service managed by procurement.

Category segmentation A method used for grouping procurement activities by related commodities and services.

Centralized A procurement system in which decision making, flow of data or goods and services, or the beginning of activities are initiated at the same central point and disseminated to remote points in the chain or organization.

Certified A supplier that does not furnish direct materials and is therefore not included on the Approved Vendor List (AVL) but who has met a particular set of requirements established by the organization. This designation might apply to a supplier removing hazardous materials or a specially licensed consultant as well as to companies that supply certain types of telecommunication or network hardware.

Collaboration The process of buyer and supplier organizations working together to achieve a common goal.

Commodity An article of commerce in a specific category of goods where each item is undifferentiated from the other.

Competition The availability of two or more unrelated suppliers seeking to gain the buyer's business.

Competitive bidding The process whereby two or more suppliers provide formal offers in order to secure the buyer's business.

Competitive negotiation Negotiations that take place following the receipt of formal offers by suppliers.

Competitive positioning The process used by a supplier to distinguish itself from its competitors.

Compliance Adherence to corporate policy and procedure as well as to government regulations and laws.

Conflict of interest A situation in which a buyer's business decisions are subordinate to personal interests.

Consignment A procedure in which one business (the consignee) accepts goods from another business (the consignor) for sale on a commission basis.

Contract A binding agreement by two or more parties that is enforceable through the legal system; the written document evidencing an agreement.

Contractor A supplier of services under contract to an organization.

COSO Committee of Sponsoring Organizations of the Treadway Commission. COSO is a framework for evaluation of internal control over financial reporting that preceded Sarbanes-Oxley.

Cosourcing The practice of performing a service jointly through internal personnel and an external supplier.

Cost The cash value of the resources used to produce or purchase a product or service.

Cost avoidance A purchasing action to ensure certain material or supplier increases is not incurred by the purchasing firm. It involves avoiding a future cost increase by delaying or reducing the impact of a proposed price increase.

Crowdsourcing An open, public request for a proposal or bids to a large group of potential suppliers.

Cultural values Concepts held by a social group that influence how members act and make choices.

Decentralized The allocation of purchasing responsibility away from a centralized purchasing department to locally dispersed departments.

Delegation of authority The formal transfer of specific authorization to exercise procurement controls from one employee in an organization to another.

Deliverable The specific item(s) or service(s) to be performed under a contract.

Design specification A specification issued to a supplier that details performance requirements as well as production methods and materials to be used.

Direct materials Materials incorporated into the product being sold.

Distribution channels A business process of storing, shipping, and transporting goods to the customer. Also describes the facilities (distribution operations, distribution centers) that conduct these activities.

Diversity suppliers Minority-owned, women-owned, and service-disabled veteran owned suppliers.

Economic conditions The overall state of the economy including supply and demand factors, employment, money supply, and balance of trade.

Electronic Data Interchange (EDI) A standardized electronic format for business to business transactions sent from one computer to another computer system, consisting of strings of data in a prearranged accepted format by both sending and receiving computer systems. See also *Value Added Network*.

Ensure supply The process used to sustain the flow of materials required by an organization.

Enterprise Resource Planning (ERP) An integrated, modular software system used to manage the important parts of an organization's operations, including product planning, purchasing parts, maintaining inventories, interacting with suppliers, providing customer service, and tracking orders.

Enterprise Risk Management (ERM) The processes and framework used by an organization to evaluate and manage business risks.

Environmental analysis The use of various techniques to monitor conditions within the environment, typically the levels of pollution and emissions.

Environmental Management System (EMS) A framework of policies and procedures used to manage the environmental consequences of an organization's activities, often using ISO 14001 guidelines.

Environmental responsibility The ethical management of the impact of an organization's activities on the external environment.

Financial analysis An assessment of an organization's financial condition to determine its stability and its capability to provide the products and services required.

Financial leverage The ability of an organization to borrow money and service its debts.

Global markets The international markets of trade available to buyers and sellers.

Global warming An increase in the temperature of Earth's atmosphere as a result of human activities that produces climate change.

Greenhouse gas Any gas in Earth's atmosphere capable of absorbing and emitting radiation that contributes to the greenhouse effect of global warming.

Hazardous material Any substance or compound that has the capability of producing adverse effects on the health and safety of human beings.

INCOTERMS A set of international shipping rules and their corresponding terminology.

Indirect materials Material used in the production process but not attributed to the production of specific saleable units.

Industrial guide A documented listing of sellers categorized by industry.

Intellectual property (IP) Unique intellectual material typically governed by patents, copyrights, trademarks, and trade secrets, IP generally refers to designs and materials owned by the originator.

International Procurement Service A third party representing the buyer's interests in purchasing from overseas locations.

Inventory Goods and materials held in stock for use in manufacturing or sale.

Invitation for Bid (IFB) Used by federal government procurement, usually for requirements over $25,000. The bidder responds with a sealed bid to be opened publicly at a stated date and time. It is primarily a price competition, and the lowest bid will win.

Joint venture The agreement of cooperation or joint ownership between two or more individuals or enterprises in a specific business enterprise rather than in a continuing relationship, as in a partnership.

Just in Time (JIT) A system and philosophy for eliminating waste by procuring, producing, and delivering the right items at the right time in the right amount. JIT typically applies to the management of inventory.

Key Performance Indicator (KPI) A measure that allows the assessment of specific performance in a given area that is critical to the overall achievement of the objective.

Lean A methodology to eliminate waste and minimize the resources needed for production.

Lean Six Sigma A system that combines lean methodologies with the reduction of process variation.

Market analysis Research of the economic conditions, suppliers, and supply and demand status in a specific category to discover capabilities and future trends.

Market conditions The characteristics of market forces in a particular industry, including supply and demand conditions, the number of competing products, the level of competitiveness, and the growth rate.

Market share The percentage of total sales within a specific market or industrial category held by an individual organization.

Market trends The direction of prices and technology within a given business category.

Master Service Agreement An agreement or contract governing the terms and conditions of the sale and purchase of specific services from a supplier.

Master Supply Agreement An agreement or contract governing the terms and conditions of the sale and purchase of specific products and services from a supplier.

Material Requirements Planning (MRP) A methodology for defining the raw material requirements for a specific product, component, or subassembly ordered by a customer or required by a business process.

Material substitution A material capable of performing in the same manner as another that can be substituted for the one in current use.

Measure of efficiency The measurement of how well any supply production or transformation process is performing.

Measure of liquidity Financial ratio of a supplier's ability to pay off its debt obligations.

Measure of profitability Supplier's profit-margin ratios: gross profit margins, operating profit margins, and net profit margins.

Minority supplier A supplier that is at least 51 percent owned by one or more citizens of the United States who are determined to be socially or economically disadvantaged.

Natural disaster An occurrence in nature that causes grievous damages, such as a hurricane, earthquake, flood, volcanic eruption, tsunami, or tornado.

Nearshoring The use of suppliers within the geographic and national proximity of the buyer; contrasts with offshoring.

Negotiation The act of discussing an issue between a buyer and a seller with the objective of reaching a mutually satisfactory agreement; bargaining.

Offshoring The relocation of supply sources to another country.

Operational alignment The condition in which all elements of an organization's operational activities are performing toward the same objective.

Opportunity analysis The process of examining ways to improve operational efficiency and profitability.

Organizational culture The beliefs and attitudes widely held and expressed by members of an organization that provide a framework for activities.

Organizational structure The manner in which an organization's reporting lines are set up to achieve its objectives.

Outsourcing The transfer of functions formerly administered and performed in-house to a supplier.

Ozone depletion The reduction of Earth's protective ozone layer in the atmosphere that filters harmful ultraviolet rays from the sun.

Partnership An agreement by buyer and supplier to collaborate and increase their joint business activity.

Performance The relative status of how well an organization is meeting its stated objectives.

Performance specifications The functional requirements for a product without stating its physical characteristics and how it should be made.

Pollution Contaminants introduced into the environment as a by-product of human activity.

Price The amount of money asked by a supplier in exchange for goods or services; the amount of money a buyer pays for a product or service.

Price cycle The increase and decrease of prices as a result of economic conditions.

Procure to Pay (P2P) Activities, transactions, and Enterprise Resource Planning system settings within the buying through settlement business cycle.

Purchasing The organizational group responsible for conducting acquisition operations.

Purchasing card (P-card) A credit card issued to employees so that they can charge preauthorized expenses directly with the provider.

Qualifiable Refers to suppliers that have been screened and meet the capability, financial, and capacity requirements for the current requirement.

These suppliers have not yet been certified or formally approved by the sourcing selection team.

Quality management A process used by organizations to ensure that its standards of quality and quality objectives are met through planning, measurement, and continuous improvement.

Raw materials The basic materials a manufacturer converts into a finished product.

Reengineering The fundamental rethinking and radical redesign of business processes to bring about dramatic improvements in an organization's operations.

Renewable habitat The dwelling place of wildlife and plants that is free of destructive human activities, degradation, or fragmentation so that it can continue to provide sustenance to its inhabitants.

Renewable resources Any natural resource that can be replenished through natural processes at a rate equal to or greater than its use. Also applies to resources that can be used without depletion, such as wind or solar power.

Request for Information (RFI) A formal document sent by a buyer to a potential supplier asking for specific information about its organization, products, and capabilities.

Request for Proposal (RFP) A formal request to a potential supplier by a buying organization outlining the available details for a particular requirement and requesting a proposal satisfying those requirements.

Request for Quotation (RFQ) A formal document including detailed specifications sent by a customer to a supplier requesting a price quotation and other specific details such as lead time.

Requirements A set of measurable user needs and wants incorporated into a project or application.

Requirements analysis A review of the Statement of Work and the corresponding development of a Work Breakdown Structure that lists all deliverables.

Reverse auction A buyer-initiated auction in which a buyer posts its product or service needs and invites real-time bids from multiple sellers with prices moving downward as vendors compete against each other. The price decreases as sellers compete for the buyer's business, with the lowest bid considered the winner.

Risk *Simple definition*: The chance of something happening that will have an adverse impact on our objectives. *More complex definition*: A measure of the inability to achieve program objectives within defined cost, schedule, and performance constraints.

Risk management The process used to assess, monitor, mitigate, control, avoid, and transfer risk.

Risk mitigation A method used to reduce or eliminate risk factors.

Risk trigger An action that sets in motion a risk event.

Sarbanes-Oxley Act (SOX) Legislation including provisions addressing audits, financial reporting and disclosure, conflicts of interest, and corporate governance at public companies. The act also establishes new supervisory mechanisms, including the new Public Company Accounting Oversight Board, for accountants and accounting firms that conduct external audits of public companies.

Scope of Work Describes in measurable detail the work to be performed under a contract or agreement as part of the Statement of Work.

Sealed bid A bid responding to an invitation by the buyer submitted in a sealed envelope to maintain confidentiality. At a designated time, all bids are opened at once.

Service Work performed by a contractor consisting primarily of labor.

Service Level Agreement (SLA) Performance measures that are part of a contract for services; defines minimum performance.

Site visit A formal visit to a supplier's facility for the purpose of qualifying the supplier to do business with the organization.

Social responsibility An obligation assumed by an organization to conduct its operations in the best interests of the society.

Solicitation An Invitation for Bids (IFB), Request for Quotation (RFQ), and Request for Proposal (RFP); a method for communicating procurement requirements and requesting responses from interested bidders.

Sourcing (strategic) The process of identifying, conducting negotiations with, and forming supply agreements with providers of goods and services.

Source to Settle (S2S) A procurement process that includes key activities: source, procure, settle, account, and analyze.

Specification(s) A clear and concise definition of technical requirements for items, materials, or services, including the criteria for determining that requirements have been met.

Spend analysis The process of categorizing and evaluating how an organization spends its funds for purchases of goods and services; typically conducted at the item level and rolled up to categories, it is used to determine areas that can produce costs savings and supplier consolidation.

Spend visibility The ability to perform accurate spend analysis, usually in real time, to monitor spending.

Standardization The process of identifying parts or services that can conform to a common specification.

Statement of Work (SOW) In a contract or contract proposal, the document that states the technical objectives, level of effort, scope, timing, and requirements of the contract. The Federal Acquisition Regulations (FAR) provides this definition:

FAR Subsection 37.602-1: Statements of work.

(a) Generally, statements of work shall define requirements in clear, concise language identifying specific work to be accomplished. Statements of work must be individually tailored to consider the period of performance, deliverable items, if any, and the desired degree of performance flexibility.

Strategic sourcing We apply the term "strategic" to the sourcing process to recognize that many sourcing projects require a long-term plan of supply chain action. It is meeting the needs of this relatively long time horizon that makes sourcing "strategic." When the word "global" is added, it means that suppliers may be selected beyond the organization's national borders.

Subcontractor A second-level contractor selected by the prime contractor awarded the contract.

Supplier certification Determines that the supplier's internal system for measurement and control of quality is sufficient to ensure it will meet the minimum quality level required without performing further incoming inspections.

Supplier evaluation Measures of supplier support, such as quality improvement and performance relative to goals, on-time delivery, and responsiveness to service requests, flexibility to accommodate late scheduling, favorable return policy, and overall reliability.

Supplier performance See *Performance.*

Supplier Relationship Management (SRM) A comprehensive approach to managing an organization's interactions with the suppliers of the goods and services it uses. The goal of SRM is to streamline and make more effective the processes between an organization and its suppliers, just as customer relationship management (CRM) is intended to streamline and make more effective the processes between an enterprise and its customers.

Supplier review A process conducted periodically with a supplier to review its immediate past performance and define operational objectives for the next period.

Supplier scorecard An evaluative report summarizing supplier performance in specific areas (such as cost, quality, and service) during a specified time and compared with prior performance, benchmarks, or goals.

Supplier selection The determination to award business to a specific supplier.

Supply base rationalization A reduction of suppliers to the minimum level required through consolidation to reduce costs and improve operations.

Supply chain The network of suppliers that move goods from the raw material state to the final consumer and ultimately to disposal.

Supply Management As defined by the Institute for Supply Management: "The identification, acquisition, access, positioning, and management of resources an organization needs or potentially needs in the attainment of its strategic objectives."

Supply positioning A process similar to spend analysis that identifies and categorizes goods and service by their relative cost and risk in order to determine the levels of staffing and talent required to manage them.

Supply risk The process that identifies elements that could cause interruption in supply for the organization.

Sustainability The ability to maintain a balance of a certain process or state in any system to ensure future availability. Today it is used most frequently in connection with biological and human systems.

Tactic The specific method and steps used to accomplish an objective.

Total Cost of Ownership (TCOO) The cumulative consideration of all the costs that might be associated with a product or service over its life span in the organization.

Toxic discharge Release of toxic pollutants into the environment.

Transactional cost The cost to an organization to process purchase transactions.

Value The worth of a product or service in relation to its cost.

Value analysis An approach to cost reduction in which components are studied carefully to determine if they can be redesigned, standardized, or made by less costly methods of production. The process attempts to define cost, quality, and customer acceptance parameters in determining the value and possible redesign or reengineering of a given function.

Value Added Network (VAN) An intermediary in the EDI process that transfers data from buyer to supplier using specialized software to enable the two to exchange information.

Work Breakdown Structure (WBS) A listing of each of the individual deliverables of a contract extracted from the Statement of Work; in project management, deliverables are listed on a timeline.

Work flow In procurement, refers to the approval steps required prior to issuing a purchase order or contract.

Suggested Reading

Chapter 1: An Overview of Global Strategic Sourcing

Global Purchasing and Supply Management: Fulfill the Vision by Victor H. Pooler, David J. Pooler, and Samuel D. Farney. Springer, 2004.

Global Sourcing: An Analysis of the Implications for Organization Design by Gerhard Trautmann. Gabler Verlag, 2008.

Global Sourcing: The Strategic Reorientation of Purchasing by Wolfgang Schneid. GRIN Verlag, 2010.

Multisourcing: Moving Beyond Outsourcing to Achieve Growth and Agility by Linda Cohen and Allie Young. Harvard Business Press, 2006.

The Procurement and Supply Manager's Desk Reference by Fred Sollish and John Semanik. John Wiley & Sons, 2007.

Purchasing Supply Management by Michiel R. Leenders, P. Fraser Johnson, Anna Flynn, and Harold E. Fearon. McGraw-Hill Education, 2009.

World Class Supply Management: The Key to Supply Chain Management by David N. Burt, Donald W. Dobler, and Stephen L. Starling. McGraw-Hill/Irwin, 2003.

Chapter 2: Operational Alignment with Sourcing Strategy

Purchasing and Supply Chain Management by Robert M. Monczka, Robert B. Handfield, and Larry Giunipero. Cengage Learning, 2008.

Purchasing Principles and Management by Peter Baily, David Farmer, David Jessop, and David Jones. Trans-Atlantic Publications, 2005.

Sourcing of Services by Lydia Bals and Evi Hartmann. Nova Publishers, 2008.

Sourcing Strategy: Principles, Policy, and Designs by Sudhi Seshadri. Springer, 2005.

The Supply Management Handbook by Joseph L. Cavinato, Anna E. Flynn, and Ralph G. Kauffman. McGraw-Hill Professional, 2006.

Supply Market Intelligence: A Managerial Handbook for Building Sourcing Strategies by Robert B. Handfield. CRC Press, 2006.

208 Suggested Reading

Chapter 3: Source to Settle (S2S)

The Procurement and Supply Manager's Desk Reference by Fred Sollish and John Semanik. John Wiley & Sons, 2007.

Purchasing and Supply Chain Management by Robert M. Monczka, Robert B. Handfield, and Larry Giunipero. Cengage Learning, 2008.

Purchasing Supply Management by Michiel R. Leenders, P. Fraser Johnson, Anna Flynn, and Harold E. Fearon. McGraw-Hill Education, 2009.

The Services Shift: Seizing the Ultimate Offshore Opportunity by Robert E. Kennedy and Ajay Sharma. FT Press, 2009.

World Class Supply Management: The Key to Supply Chain Management by David N. Burt, Donald W. Dobler, and Stephen L. Starling. McGraw-Hill/Irwin, 2003.

Chapter 4: Cultural Considerations for Global Sourcing

Case Studies in Japanese Negotiating Behavior by Michael Blaker, Paul Giarra, and Ezra F. Vogel. U.S. Institute of Peace Press, 2002.

China Now: Doing Business in the World's Most Dynamic Market by N. Mark Lam and John Graham. McGraw-Hill, 2006.

The Conflict Resolution Source (a guide to international forms of conflict resolution). www.crinfo.org/action/search-portal.jsp?pid=1889&nid=2309.

Doing Business in China: How to Profit in the World's Fastest Growing Market by Ted Plafker. Business Plus, 2008.

Executive Planet (business culture guide). www.executiveplanet.com/index.php?title=Main_Page.

Global Sourcing: Opportunities for the Future: China, India, Eastern Europe: How to Benefit from the Potential of International Procurement by Gerd Kerkhoff. Wiley-VCH, 2006.

Global Sourcing—Procurement in China by Hauke Jensen. GRIN Verlag, 2009.

The Handbook of Negotiation and Culture by Michele J. Gelfand and Jeanne M. Brett. Stanford University Press, 2004.

ITIM International (a very thorough cross-reference of the cultural values of many countries). www.geert-hofstede.com.

Low-Cost Country Sourcing: Trends and Implications by Martin Lockström. DUV, 2007.

Managing Cultural Differences: Global Leadership Strategies for the 21st Century by Robert T. Moran, Philip Robert Harris, and Sarah Virgilia Moran. Butterworth-Heinemann, 2007.

The Procurement and Supply Manager's Desk Reference by Fred Sollish and John Semanik. John Wiley & Sons, 2007.

"Resource Guide for Researching Intellectual Property Law in an International Context," by Andrew Larrick, 2008. http://library.law .columbia.edu/guides/International_intellectual_property.

"United Nations Convention on Contracts for the International Sale of Goods," 1980. www.cisg.law.pace.edu/cisg/countries/cntries.html. A downloadable .pdf file is available at: www.uncitral.org/pdf/english/ texts/sales/cisg/CISG.pdf.

"World Business Culture." www.worldbusinessculture.com.

"World Intellectual Property Organization." www.wipo.int/portal/index .html.en.

Chapter 5: Supplier Research and Market Analysis

The Alignment Performance Link in Purchasing and Supply Management by Christian Baier. Gabler Verlag, 2008.

The Procurement and Supply Manager's Desk Reference by Fred Sollish and John Semanik. John Wiley & Sons, 2007.

Purchasing and Supply Chain Management by Robert M. Monczka, Robert B. Handfield, and Larry Giunipero. Cengage Learning, 2008.

Purchasing and Supply Chain Management: Analysis, Strategy, Planning and Practice by Arjan Van Weele. Cengage Learning EMEA, 2009.

The Supply-Based Advantage: How to Link Suppliers to Your Organization's Corporate Strategy by Stephen C. Rogers. AMACOM Division, American Management Association, 2009.

The Supply Management Handbook by Joseph L. Cavinato, Anna E. Flynn, and Ralph G. Kauffman. McGraw-Hill Professional, 2006.

World Class Supply Management: The Key to Supply Chain Management by David N. Burt, Donald W. Dobler, and Stephen L. Starling. McGraw-Hill/Irwin, 2003.

Chapter 6: Solicitation of Bids and Proposals

Handbook of Procurement by Nicola Dimitri, Gustavo Piga, and Giancarlo Spagnolo. Cambridge University Press, 2006.

The Procurement and Supply Manager's Desk Reference by Fred Sollish and John Semanik. John Wiley & Sons, 2007.

Purchasing Supply Management by Michiel R. Leenders, P. Fraser Johnson, Anna Flynn, Harold E. Fearon. McGraw-Hill Education, 2009.

The Sourcing Solution: A Step-by-Step Guide to Creating a Successful Purchasing Program by Larry Paquette. AMACOM Division, American Management Association, 2004.

World Class Supply Management: The Key to Supply Chain Management by David N. Burt, Donald W. Dobler, and Stephen L. Starling. McGraw-Hill/Irwin, 2003.

Chapter 7: Supplier Evaluation and Selection

Managing the Global Supply Chain by Tage Skjott-Larsen and Philip B. Schary. Copenhagen Business School Press DK, 2007.

The Procurement and Supply Manager's Desk Reference by Fred Sollish and John Semanik. John Wiley & Sons, 2007.

Principles of Supply Chain Management by Joel D. Wisner, Keah-Choon Tan, and G. Keong Leong. Cengage Learning, 2008.

Proven Solutions for Improving Supply Chain Performance by C. Carl Pegels. IAP, 2005.

Strategic Purchasing and Supply Management: A Strategy-based Selection of Suppliers by Roger Moser. Springer, 2007.

Supply Chain Excellence: A Handbook for Dramatic Improvement Using The SCOR Model by Peter Bolstorff and Robert G. Rosenbaum. AMACOM Division, American Management Association, 2007.

Supply Chain Management: Processes, Partnerships, Performance by Douglas M. Lambert. Supply Chain Management Institute, 2008.

World Class Supply Management: The Key to Supply Chain Management by David N. Burt, Donald W. Dobler, and Stephen L. Starling. McGraw-Hill/Irwin, 2003.

Chapter 8: Negotiation Revisited

Anybody Can Negotiate—Even You!: How to Become a Master Negotiator by Michael Geraghty. iUniverse, 2006.

Case Studies in Japanese Negotiating Behavior by Michael Blaker, Paul Giarra, and Ezra F. Vogel. U.S. Institute of Peace Press, 2002.

The Handbook of Negotiation and Culture by Michele J. Gelfand and Jeanne M. Brett. Stanford University Press, 2004.

Negotiation Boot Camp: How to Resolve Conflict, Satisfy Customers, and Make Better Deals by Ed Brodow. Broadway Business, 2006.

The Only Negotiating Guide You'll Ever Need: 101 Ways to Win Every Time in Any Situation by Peter B. Stark and Jane Flaherty. Broadway, 2003.

The Procurement and Supply Manager's Desk Reference by Fred Sollish and John Semanik. John Wiley & Sons, 2007.

Purchasing Supply Management by Michiel R. Leenders, P. Fraser Johnson, Anna Flynn, and Harold E. Fearon. McGraw-Hill Education, 2009.

World Class Supply Management: The Key to Supply Chain Management by David N. Burt, Donald W. Dobler and Stephen L. Starling. McGraw-Hill/Irwin, 2003.

Chapter 9: Supplier Diversity

The Diversity Scorecard: Evaluating the Impact of Diversity on Organizational Performance by Edward E. Hubbard. Butterworth-Heinemann, 2004.

The Procurement and Supply Manager's Desk Reference by Fred Sollish and John Semanik. John Wiley & Sons, 2007.

Purchasing and Supply Chain Management by Robert M. Monczka, Robert B. Handfield, and Larry Giunipero. Cengage Learning, 2008.

Straight to the Bottom Line: An Executive's Roadmap to World Class Supply Management by Robert A. Rudzki, Douglas A. Smock, and Michael Katzorke. J. Ross Publishing, 2005.

Strategies for Generating E-Business Returns on Investment by Namchul Shin. Idea Group Inc. (IGI), 2005.

World Class Supply Management: The Key to Supply Chain Management by David N. Burt, Donald W. Dobler, and Stephen L. Starling. McGraw-Hill/Irwin, 2003.

Chapter 10: Sustainability

Best Practice Procurement: Public and Private Sector Perspectives by Andrew Erridge, Ruth Fee, and John McIlroy. Gower Publishing, 2001.

Closed-Loop Supply Chains: New Developments to Improve the Sustainability of Business Practices by Mark E. Ferguson and Gilvan C. Souza. Auerbach Publications, 2010.

Essentials of Business Ethics: Creating an Organization of High Integrity and Superior Performance by Denis Collins. John Wiley & Sons, 2009.

Fix Your Supply Chain: How to Create a Sustainable Lean Improvement Roadmap by Paul Husby and Dan Swartwood. Productivity Press.

Purchasing and Supply Chain Management: Analysis, Strategy, Planning and Practice by Arjan Van Weele. Cengage Learning EMEA, 2009.

Sustainable Strategic Management by W. Edward Stead, Jean Garner Stead, and Mark Starik. M.E. Sharpe, 2009.

21st Century Management: A Reference Handbook, Volume 1 by Charles Wankel. SAGE, 2008.

Chapter 11: Risk

Low-Cost Country Sourcing: Trends and Implications by Martin Lockström. DUV, 2007.

Essentials of Financial Risk Management by Karen A. Horcher. John Wiley & Sons, 2005.

Global Sourcing and Purchasing Post 9/11 by Michael Assaf, Cynthia Bonincontro, and Stephen Johnsen. J. Ross Publishing, 2005.

Global Sourcing Logistics: How to Manage Risk and Gain Competitive Advantage in a Worldwide Marketplace by Thomas A. Cook. AMACOM Division, American Management Association, 2007.

Managing Global Supply and Risk: Best Practices, Concepts, and Strategies by Robert J. Trent and Llewellyn Roberts. J. Ross Publishing, 2009.

Managing Global Supply Chains: Compliance, Security, and Dealing with Terrorism by Thomas A. Cook. CRC Press, 2008.

The Procurement and Supply Manager's Desk Reference by Fred Sollish and John Semanik. John Wiley & Sons, 2007.

Purchasing Supply Management by Michiel R. Leenders, P. Fraser Johnson, Anna Flynn, and Harold E. Fearon. McGraw-Hill Education, 2009.

Single Point of Failure: The 10 Essential Laws of Supply Chain Risk Management by Gary S. Lynch. John Wiley & Sons, 2009.

Supply Chain Risk: A Handbook of Assessment, Management, and Performance by George A. Zsidisin and Bob Ritchie. Springer US, 2009.

Supply Chain Risk Management: Minimizing Disruptions in Global Sourcing by Robert Handfield and Kevin P. McCormack. Auerbach Publications, 2007.

Supply Chain Risk Management: Vulnerability and Resilience in Logistics by Donald Waters. Kogan Page, 2007.

World Class Supply Management: The Key to Supply Chain Management by David N. Burt, Donald W. Dobler, and Stephen L. Starling. McGraw-Hill/Irwin, 2003.

Chapter 12: Global Sourcing

Doing Business in China: How to Profit in the World's Fastest Growing Market by Ted Plafker. Business Plus, 2008.

Doing Business in China for Dummies by Robert Collins and Carson Block. John Wiley & Sons, 2007.

42 Rules for Sourcing and Manufacturing in China by Rosemary Coates and Laura Lowell. Super Star Press, 2009.

The Handbook of International Trade and Finance by Anders Grath. Kogan Page, 2008.

Import/Export for Dummies by John J. Capela. John Wiley & Sons, 2008.

Low-Cost Country Sourcing: Trends and Implications by Martin Lockström. DUV, 2007.

Supply Chain Management Best Practices by David Blanchard. John Wiley & Sons, 2010.

About the Authors

Fred Sollish, MS is the Managing Director of eParagon, LLC, a consulting firm specializing in providing training and working tools for the supply chain management profession. Fred is former President and CEO of the Institute for Supply Management (ISM) Silicon Valley affiliate. He also is an instructor for sourcing, supply management, and purchasing-related courses for various worldwide corporations and governmental organizations. Fred also produces and manages an online program in strategic sourcing for the Center for Intelligent Design Networks at the University of Texas, Dallas and a similar program offered to the public independently at http://:supplyknowledge.coggno.com.

John Semanik, MBA is Cofounder and Director of eParagon, LLC. He has served in senior corporate supply chain management positions at such leading-edge companies as Hewlett-Packard, Sun Microsystems (acquired by Oracle), and Xilinx, Inc. John was Founder, the Managing Director, and an instructor for San Jose State University's Professional Development curriculum in supply chain management and purchasing. He serves on the Board of Directors of the Institute for Supply Management (ISM) Silicon Valley affiliate.

Index